T0208990

Reborn as the Self

How to Shed Your Identity, Contain Your Mind
and Become the Creator of the Life You Desire

*A guide to Inner Management based on real life experiences
and including practical tools and exercises.*

PAOLA CORINALDESI

BALBOA.
PRESS
A DIVISION OF HAY HOUSE

Balboa Press books may be ordered through booksellers or by contacting:

Balboa Press
A Division of Hay House
1663 Liberty Drive
Bloomington, IN 47403
www.balboapress.com
1 (877) 407-4847

Print information available on the last page.

ISBN: 978-1-9822-0697-0 (sc)
ISBN: 978-1-9822-0698-7 (hc)
ISBN: 978-1-9822-0699-4 (e)

Library of Congress Control Number: 2018907336

Balboa Press rev. date: 07/11/2018

CONTENTS

Introduction..vii

Chapter 1 Growing Up as a Survivor.................................1
Chapter 2 From Compulsion to Awareness 22
Chapter 3 The Importance of Assuming Responsibility 38
Chapter 4 Heaven is a State of Mind: Mind & Co...................49
Chapter 5 Entanglement: My Biggest Challenge.....................60
Chapter 6 Acceptance: The Shortcut to Enlightenment...........69
Chapter 7 Learning to Love 75
Chapter 8 About Compassion..87
Chapter 9 Fear and Me..97
Chapter 10 Self-Love and Radical Acceptance........................115
Chapter 11 What If Our Life Purpose is Connection?.............131
Chapter 12 What I Have Come to Understand........................143

Conclusion: Living from the Space of the Self...................153
Afterword: The Subtle Play of Life and Death.....................159
Acknowledgements...165
About the Author..169
Appendix I: Finding a Yoga Center 171

INTRODUCTION

"I know you're tired but come, this is the way."- Rumi

As I think about this book and how it came to be, a profound sense of reverence flows through me, for the amazing perfection—and absolute fragility—of this masterpiece called life.

This book is the manifestation in form of my longing and seeking; it is the result of my journey from identity to self and the proof that if we consciously decide to live from the space of our true self, we can live without suffering and literally create the life we desire.

Let me tell you how it came to be written.

Some years ago, while mentally scrolling through scenes from my life, I saw an unhappy and frustrated woman. She had raised a child almost completely on her own, working nine to six her entire life and watching the world turn around her without being a part of it. She was imprisoned within the safe walls of self-preservation; though life continued on outside, inside this fortress of her own making, she already felt dead.

I was this woman, trapped in identity and psychological reality while real life passed by—until the day I realized that there must be something more to life than just surviving and functioning.

Up until that day, I was merely a survivor. My story is of a woman who expanded into the external world through a corporate job, money, family, traditional view of success, identified herself totally in her story (identity), became imprisoned in her own comfort zone, and found herself feeling dead while still living.

Life had to shake me up to bring me toward awareness. It did so ruthlessly.

I had to lose everything: my family, my health, my father. I also had to face the terrifying possibility of losing someone else: my gentlest friend and truest mirror, my beloved daughter.

I had lost track of myself. I was enveloped in suffering and I could not see a way out.

My cyclical, repetitive mental patterns, my identification with them and with my story (identity) had to perish before I could start living a new, joyful existence out of my true self. I had to find a joy from within that no person or situation outside can ever affect.

I ended up with an existence built on pure love and compassion for others and myself, where success means that I am the creator of everything I desire and long for, and where my decisions come from a place of love for myself rather than fear.

I waded across life in search of transformation, only to come to the realization that my concept of love was not love, my concept of death was not death and my concept of life was not real life at all.

From a purely functional, compulsive, fearful and conditioned identity who lived mostly within her self-created psychological reality, I transformed myself into a free, fearless, aware and joyful being who resides in the beauty and grace of its own self.

I had to metaphorically die while living to find my way back home; a death which was not of the body, but of my mind, beliefs, judgments, thoughts and emotions. In short, I had to face the death of the concept of me.

I still can remember the morning at work when, without planning it at all, I stood up and went to speak with my boss. I had spent most of the previous days unhappy at my desk, and suddenly a voice within, a force of some type, pushed me to act. I remember how I silently and fearfully walked across the office without really knowing what I was going to say. Then I heard myself calmly and firmly state, "I want to request a sabbatical year." Though I expected resistance, I was astonished to hear my boss answer, "Okay. Let's see how to shift your projects; if you need time off, you can take it."

In that exact moment, it felt like a stone had fallen from my heart. I realized that I had been searching for a way to break out of my non-life without knowing how to do so. It was not a typical mid-life crisis decision, where changing to another place and different circumstances would have been enough. I was truly seeking for transformation. I needed ample time and silence to look inward and merge with my true essence.

I temporarily left my job, rented my house and moved to Mauritius with the firm intention to only *be*.

I lived near the ocean with only nature around me—something that had long been one of my heart's desires. I gave myself the freedom of living at my own pace, of slowing down from the frenetic rhythm of modern life. I did daily yoga, meditation and writing; I took enough time for friends and life, giving them my fullest attention. I travelled to India, where I volunteered in a children's school while my mentor, best friend and most sincere mirror showed me the way to freedom and inner joy.

I lived simply and happily, one hundred percent involved in everything I did and doing things that really mattered to me.

It was during this time that this book was born. My daily writing, done without any intention of writing a book, turned out later to be my gift and contribution to all the people, who, like me, were looking for answers. The more I wrote down what I thought, felt and experienced, the more I realized that there were many people there outside who could be helped by it; people who had the same longing and the same thirst; people who were looking for practical tools to break their own conditioning and become creators of the life they desired.

I went through so many challenges in my life and I learned so much from them that I feel it is my responsibility to share this awareness and wisdom with you. There are so many people who are facing or will have to face the same challenges that I did, and if I can help save them from having to suffer unnecessarily—if I can quicken their path to an increased awareness and the life they always desired without needing a lifetime—I am more than honored to do so.

So, please consider this book a gift from me for this generation and the ones to come. It is a gift for all those who are longing for and open to true transformation. I don't want the experience and awareness of a lifetime to be a waste. I don't want it to remain trapped within the limited boundaries of my person. It is my wish to spread it to everyone that is consciously or unconsciously seeking it.

I want everyone to know that there is a way to find true happiness and become the creator of the life one desires—a way which can spare lots of unnecessary suffering, and which doesn't necessarily have to take a lifetime to come to fruition.

Every page of this book is the result of lifelong conversations with my self and my meditations about the ego, the mind and its destructive power; love and our incapacity to let it free; relationships; children; and death. It describes my expansion from self, in which we naturally abode during childhood, to identity, the conditioning we take up during adulthood—and then back home to the self, which is the next level entirely. I came to this after having realized that everything I was longing for—money, career, relationships, family—were only illusory surrogates for my happiness. They weren't true life, the one that was burning within me to be heard, loved and revealed against all odds.

This book is the result of my sadness, desperation and confusion, transformed into love for myself and for other human beings; of my anger, aggression and resentment, transformed into understanding and compassion for the human nature and condition; of years of anxieties, fears and unanswered questions, transformed into radical acceptance of my being, life, and everything that is.

This book is the path of life of a little girl who had to put forth strenuous effort to be loved and accepted the way she was, who lost herself to please others, who made herself unimportant and invisible. A little girl who became identified with too many people and things, who got lost and found her way back home at the age of 50. This didn't happen suddenly, but after a process that was strongly initiated, wanted and longed for; after a strenuous process of self-observation, self-love and radical acceptance of herself and life.

This book is the result of a myriad of other books that I gorged upon in the hope of finding something more than the petit physicality of life. It is the result of my conversations with my beloved mentor and of the teachings imparted to me by my own fears and my false sense of loneliness as I searched for something that seemed so far away, but which has always been right there, inside of me. Something which is a no-thing with no form and is the true me.

I started writing this book a million times and I stopped a million times, too. My thoughts kept me from writing and sharing my story and wisdom with you. They told me that I was not special enough to give advice to others and questioned whether I could really be of help to anyone. As you see, my mind was trying to preserve my safety by not allowing things to happen—because when things happen, we transform, and the mind doesn't like transformation at all. By raising all kinds of doubts, my mind was preventing me from having a whole, magic life, expressing and sharing my experiences and being of help for others.

It was only when I reached a certain degree of awareness, and after I learned to accept and love myself radically, that all my doubts dissolved and I felt the necessary love, compassion and responsibility to reveal such personal contents about my life with the vision of being of help. It is my will and my commitment in helping people get out of suffering and entering a space of joy and wellbeing that gives me the courage to write the story of releasing my Identity and the teachings I gained from doing so.

My journey was a long one and it could start only when I realized that the way in is the only way out; when I understood that joy must be sculpted and nourished from within, as this is where it comes from; that I, and only I, am responsible for choosing happiness over misery. It all started when I realized that I had to gain back that space within me, my authentic self and essence, knowing that if I reside there, I reside in pure joy and peace, regardless of the situation outside.

Learning to manage my inner experience was fundamental to me. It has taught me how to observe my mind and emotions without becoming identified with them; how to ignore negative thought patterns by consciously refusing to give them my energy; how to understand where my pain-body and all the false beliefs about myself and others came from; how to manage my emotions and understand that fears were created when I identified with my negative thoughts; last but not least, it led me to manifest everything I truly desire in life. Eventually, I organized a training program that reflects this, called Inner Management.

Today, I have freed my mind of all unnecessary thoughts, emotions and beliefs, and I can use my energy to create and sculpt my life exactly the way I want it. My focus and perception on things and people have heightened to a level that I can be one hundred percent present with the persons I meet and do the things that matter most to me. As a result, I am effortlessly happy in my relationships as well as in everything else I do. Of course, I cannot control or change what people want and like to think about me and in general, but I can avoid lots of suffering by remaining true to my authentic self. I got rid of almost all my unnecessary, life-neglecting fears, and consequently my stress level is nearly nonexistent; I have learned to dwell, most of the time, in the present moment and in the essence of my self. Though my journey is not yet complete, it's my heart's desire to share it with you.

My transformation it is not a miracle! It is something that every human being can reach. If I could do it, you can do it! Of course, it is an evolutionary journey, and as such, it never truly reaches its end. When we think we have overcome all of our fears, something will happen to strengthen us and make sure we stick to the stability of our self, no matter what happens. All situations that life throws at us are stepping stones toward freedom—we simply need to be willing to accept them without resistance and live them from the place of our stable self.

So, we only need to let go of our resistance, get started, turn inward and realize that we are the creator of our own life and responsible for our own inner happiness. This is all it takes!

I am convinced that no major change can happen on the outside (world peace, religious conflicts, hunger) unless we learn to manage our inside. Global change starts with the transformation of human consciousness at individual level, because we are society, and what society becomes is us. So, let us be the ones who kick off this global transformation by taking responsibility for our individual happiness and wellbeing. Let us be the ones who walk the path from dis-ease to ease, from ambition to vision, from management to leadership.

May you shed your identity, contain your mind, and blossom into a free and joyful being who is the creator of your own life and vision! May my story help you discover your true self, merge with it and live from that space.

"In your light I learn how to love. In your beauty how to make poems. You dance inside my chest, where no one sees you. But sometimes I do, and that sight becomes this art." - Rumi

My transformation has blessed my life, and with the same love and generosity with which my knowledge was transferred to me, I want to share it with all of you.

Before starting to read the book, is essential that you understand three terms that are used frequently: self, identity and awareness. Let me explain you what I mean when I use them.

By *self*, I mean the pure intelligence within us, an intelligence free from thoughts, emotions and memories. This powerful essence or pure intelligence, which is you, can also be defined as spirit, soul, being, intuition, energy, creative power or God. As some of those terms have been charged in the past with misleading spiritual and religious meanings, I prefer to use the word *self* as denomination for the non-physical part of human beings. This essence has no form and can only be perceived through enhanced awareness and perception.

The term *identity* means the external accumulation of beliefs, opinions, prejudices, philosophies and all the conditioning we have gathered throughout our life. Identity also includes the body (accumulation of food) and the mind (accumulation of impressions, beliefs, and opinions). You'll notice that both are accumulations gathered from the outside.

I also sometimes define identity in the book as ego, persona or story. All of those terms refer to the personal story gathered during a life-time which contribute to identity.

Being a physical form, the identity is subjected to changes and consequently to the impermanence of life; furthermore, the identity has a limited perception of life, as it can only make use of the five senses to perceive. I refer to the identity as the limited part of a being and to the self as the limitless energy/intelligence within every being.

The third frequently recurrent term in the book is *awareness*. I use it in the sense of become conscious of something through real experience. Knowledge, which we grasp intellectually, is not awareness. Awareness is the conscious understanding of oneself or of a reality through personal experience. The terms *awareness* and *consciousness* are used interchangeably in this book.

I suggest that you read the book chapter by chapter, in sequence. Each chapter is based on a real-life situation I experienced, and as I describe each one, I transfer a new principle of Inner Management, giving you practical tools and methods that are crucial for your internal wellbeing and transformation. They will light your life and provide you with joyous surprises, a profound sense of abundance, magic, peace and creativity.

Please note that you do not have to rush through this book. It's better to take your time, understanding each chapter and principle correctly, than to push through anxiously, working in the wrong direction.

I suggest that you keep this book as a guide at hand and read the needed chapters again, depending on the life situations and challenges you are going through. Apply the tools and practices in your daily life as much as it is possible for you; remember that if a practice seems too difficult for you to do in certain moments of your life, these are the exact moments when the practice can be of most use.

I kindly advise you not to read this book and do the practices with too much effort. Do not force yourself to do anything, as you are whole the way you are! Only if you love seeking, understanding and practicing, take the book in your hand, enjoy it and stay open for the quantum shift it will bring into your life!

I assure you that this book can transform you into a joyful and successful being, free from all conditioning and suffering. It worked for me, and it will for you too! You simply need to stay open, let it happen and take some time for yourself to integrate the new practices and positive habits into your daily routine. Simply enjoy the path!

I am a seeker and I write for seekers; for all those who want to break down the walls they have built for self-preservation, the conditioning of society, the patterns of their own mind, their identity and all the concepts they believe in, and transform themselves into free, joyful and powerful beings. I write for all those who know that there is more to life than just surviving;

that life is the canvas on which creation sketched us, in order to evolve our consciousness and transform us from survivors to creators, from a sketch into a beautiful vibrant painting, from a seed into a beautiful tree, with unlimited possibilities for growth.

It is my wish and my blessing that by reading this book, you can learn to flow with life and be the creator of your own reality, because each of us attracts only what we desperately long to experience.

Chapter I

GROWING UP AS A SURVIVOR

**"You were born with wings, why prefer
to crawl through life?" - Rumi**

From the authentic space of my self, I look at my story.
I see a little girl, very solar, spontaneous and intelligent; she
loves being in the nature and playing with dogs and cats; she
often feels alone; she wants to play, but she can't get attention;
everything seems to be more important than her, in her eyes at
least; she lies on her bed, playing with her cat; she feels lonely.
Sometimes she goes out in the yard and plays with her cousins
and brother; other times, she spends hours playing with paper
dolls, creating colored, vibrant dresses out of paper. She loves
drawing and she adores colors. She likes to sing and dance. I
see a strange atmosphere; sometimes she is fearful, and she tries
to stand up for her rights but does not have much success. She
gives up.

She decides to become perfect in the hope that somebody
will give her attention and appreciation—or at least notice her.
She notices positive reactions to her attempt at perfection. I see
a girl who sets very high expectations for herself and criticizes
herself every time she isn't able to be better than she is. She

doesn't know yet that perfection doesn't exist. She is convinced that she will gain love, acceptance and understanding by being perfect. I see lots of sadness, effort, struggle, disillusionment and resignation.

Nevertheless, she is a powerful fighter, highly disciplined, and intelligent enough to successfully gain a university degree, become professional and well known in the world of judo and athletics. She marries her first husband, builds a family and starts her own life.

She lives her life, expanding and experiencing lots of happiness.

She doesn't know yet that her home is love. Instead, she creates a false home built on weak foundations—lack of self-love, attachment to loved ones, fears and neediness. This false home will soon crash.

I was born a very intelligent, solar child and, like everybody, started wearing my identity in the moment they gave me a name. My environment taught me quickly how to survive and get to material security.

Directly or indirectly, I was taught that life is a struggle; that the world is a dangerous place where we need to work hard to survive. I learned that happiness is not my birthright but something I had to struggle hard for. In short, happiness seemed to be a luxury for a few lucky people. My motto was "work hard," instead of "work happily."

I learned very well how to be a good survivor in society. I understood early enough that if I wanted to be accepted, I needed to fit in.

I always felt a longing to express and experience my passions and talents. I loved Latin standard dancing as a child, and I still do; I was fascinated by the way two human bodies could express grace in movement. When I watched others dance, I felt like a little child who, with widely open eyes, wonders about the life around him while trying to discover it.

I wished I could have learned one day to move my body in that way, like a piece of life in ecstatic motion—legs, hips, arms, shoulders and head perfectly aligned like a well-attuned instrument releasing a perfect, graceful sound. I loved how the colorful, vivid dresses of the dancing women waved in the air; they looked like Goddesses in a sacred dance. I wanted to be one of them one day!

Unfortunately, arts, dancing and singing were not deemed important in an environment which was merely based on security, and consequently were not cultivated. Studying the arts or doing anything for the nourishment of our true self was, at best, something considered nice—never necessary. It was time-wasting entertainment compared to the real goal: survival, which meant studying for the sake of money.

In this way, my natural longing for the things that set my heart on fire was completely overshadowed by the concept of earning money, surviving and creating a safe life.

This is why today, I consider it vital that we never lose touch with our true passions and talents—that we stay connected to everything our true self longs for.

At this point, I would like to encourage everybody to drop the habit of teaching children to study for the sake of money. I know in my skin that this only creates unhappy beings. Instead, we can teach them to follow and nourish their true talents. The heightened focus on money is also the reason why, in my opinion, societies no longer create any great geniuses. Where are the Leonardo's, the Michelangelo's, the Tesla's or Edison's?

They were all great thinkers who gave themselves the time to unfold and work on what they truly, passionately loved; they spent their lives following their passions, ending up becoming geniuses who made it pretty well through life too.

Our society, in contrast, is full of too many beings who have to practically prostitute themselves in a job that doesn't fit them; a job that doesn't help them thrive because it doesn't match their talents and was only chosen in the name of some sort of God that is synonymous with money. We have the best technologies and the highest level of wealth compared to previous generations, yet we are certainly not the happiest and most fulfilled generation.

This partially explains why so many of us are suffering from stress, depression and dis-ease of all kinds: not only do we force ourselves to spend every day doing something that doesn't match our talents and passions, but we invest huge effort into trying to be exceptionally good at it!

Instead, we should live in a society that offers us a great environment in which to blossom as human beings; it should offer the terrain to enhance our talents and creativity. As it is now, society only uses human beings to support an economical system based on the wealth of a few rich families, sculpting human beings into "mass beings" and leveling out their uniqueness, instead of supporting individuality (from Latin: *Individuum*, meaning indivisible entity, one).

Getting back to my story, I was born, like all of us, with this great gift of instinctively knowing, how to be effortlessly happy and enjoy everything that is. Many others felt this way, too. As little children we knew how to spend time alone without feeling lonely. At the same time, we were totally immersed— one hundred percent involved—in the liveliness of life and all those around us. No fears, no doubts, judgments or critics; less dualism and more oneness and harmony.

Nature, play, love, hate, friendship, betrayal, creativity, risk, comfort, success, failure, justice, injustice, win, loss, good and evil—all the dualities of life were experienced without drama and wounds. As children we fell, stood up, smiled and went on with full involvement, eager to discover life. None of us lost any time evaluating the situation intellectually, judging ourselves as a failure and creating wrong beliefs about ourselves. We knew how to learn from a mistake or situation without getting fully wounded and shattered because of it.

Unfortunately, during the course of life, we lost this great capability of simply being and started taking everything as utterly personal. Why? Because of the mind and the conditioned identity. We create a layer of accumulated impressions, memories, opinions and beliefs around our being. Then we identify with that layer, thinking seriously that it is us.

Look back at your childhood and ask yourself: how was your experience?

Were you not more exuberant, sincere, open, perceptive, creative, and simply happier? The answer is the same for all of us: we were all more inclusive, we were able to incorporate everybody and everything in our experience without fears and doubts.

Now let's have a look at who we have become; maybe not all of us, but most of us have become more *exclusive*, meaning we see ourselves and others, good and bad, failure and success. We live completely in the dual nature of our physical and psychological Identity.

Since dualities separate, oneness/inclusiveness unites. I call this oneness *inclusiveness*, meaning our capacity to see and embrace every creature we meet as part of ourselves.

With an exclusive attitude, we separate ourselves from everybody and everything. We live in our rich houses and in our comfort zone, not noticing that we are isolating ourselves even from life itself. Our walls of preservation and safety have also become our walls of imprisonment. Rates of depression and isolation have never been as high as they are today, despite our material wealth and our high technology standards.

As far as I am concerned, all my child-like qualities and my true self became shadowed due to external conditioning. I was taught that my spontaneity was not good because it wasn't in line with the standard behavior, that happiness carried a kind of danger and it was not good for me to dwell in it; that sexuality was a sin, if freely expressed; that as a girl, I had to feel inadequate; that life is a dangerous place I must fear; and that to dwell in the state of being equals to laziness, while only doing is good.

The conditioning starts when we are called by our name for the first time; this is the beginning of the identity. Later on, this identity is fed by all kind of notions, opinions, judgments and impressions, with which we identify to the point that we believe it to be our true self when in reality, nothing is further from the truth. It's no wonder that my true, child-like self became quiescent during the course of life, substituted by a mind constantly at work in its loyal attempt to preserve my identity at all costs. This is how I became an identity, completely losing contact with my true self, my dreams and visions, and the real life outside.

Why do we believe of being the identity, knowing that this is only an accumulation of teachings, beliefs, opinions, and the conditioning gathered from the outside during the course of our lives?

Why do we believe we are our mind, rather than our true self?

Everything which is accumulated from outside can belong to us—but it cannot *be* us!

We can think because we exist in the first place, and not the other way around. It is only because we are a piece of life that we have the capacity to think. The education system, family, religious and social institutions of all kinds have conditioned us to the point of making us believe that their version of truth is the real truth. When we look closer, we can see that family, church and school have completely failed in their teachings! Nevertheless, they keep making us believe that what didn't work for them and their success will surely work for us!

We have been converted into beings which can only survive in society. The price we paid was the loss of our creativity and our happiness, which puts us far away from being realized beings. We eat, sleep, copulate, work, function and repeat these rituals every day of our life up until our death. Most of our lives contain no trace of expressing our limitless potential to the fullest!

We have everything but we don't have time. Time has become the most precious good we long for, but in the society we actually live in, we are not allowed to have it. Is this happiness? Surely not.

Some readers may be thinking, "What is wrong with wanting to be only a survivor?" The truth is that there is nothing wrong with it; it is only a very limited way of living. I know that we, as human beings, are the only species to have been created with such an endless potential, that it would be a shame not to explore it during the course of a lifetime! For a dog or another animal to live as a survivor is fine, but human beings are the only species to have been equipped not only with limitless capabilities, but also with the free will to decide how to use them.

Our potential deserves and longs to be explored and experienced in this life!

We fear our endless possibilities and by doing so, we imprison ourselves within the safe limits of our comfort zone, our well-known habits and rituals.

Believe me, I know what I am talking about because I was a survivor for most of my life; one of the reasons why I am writing this book is to awaken people from the trance of believing to be their identity. It's not worth wasting a lifetime to realize it! It's true that as long as we live in a society, we have to make use of our identity, but we have to realize that it is not our true self and that we can slip in and out of it whenever we want—and especially when it's keeping us trapped into a life we actually never wanted.

As far as my life is concerned, I did the best use of my survivor-capabilities, reaching what we erroneously call "success" early on in life. I continued accumulating material wealth and social achievements until I woke up one morning and became aware that all those things and achievements which defined me, were of no-existential value.

I had everything, but I had nothing. I was unhappy.

Of course, I had moments that weren't so bad. Each time I achieved something new, I was happy for a little while, but soon thereafter, I was looking for the next achievement and action plan. And once I had a new plan, of course I was not happy, until I reached the goal. I was always longing for more, trapped in the rat race until I asked myself: How much would be enough? The stars? The entire galaxy? Maybe the universe?

I became a functioning unit, working every day the entire day and as soon as I came home, I kept working—not with the things I loved, but the things that I had to take care of.

Unconsciously, I had already stopped living, safe within my wealthy castle, waiting for my pension.

I grew up trying to attract love and attention through being successful. I was a judo professional and always at the top of my class at school. I got a university degree with the highest score within a short period of time. I got jobs in the best multinational companies. I got money, success, a family. Doesn't it sound like a perfectly happy and successful identity?

Perhaps it does, but it was not.

As it turned out, the longing that I felt for wealth and success, which pushed me to expand as an identity, was in reality a longing for inner freedom and for the expression of the limitless creative power within. I simply didn't realize it at the time.

I sensed that the meaning of life couldn't be only material things, family and a social identity. I sensed that there must be more to it. But I was too busy and worried about preserving my safety and identity to take the time to stop and look inward.

Does this sound familiar?

I was following my ambition instead of my vision, losing sight of how I really wanted to live and who I loved to be; I became purely functional, endlessly residing in the madness of my mental construct.

Please don't misunderstand me. There is nothing wrong about wanting a family and a certain social security if it is done consciously and doesn't turn you into a slave to your own objectives. What I am talking about is choosing out of fear instead of self-love, when we are identified in our objectives to the point that we become imprisoned by our own desires and become blind to freedom and true happiness. When this happens, we must realize that life is the path to the objective, rather than the objective itself. This means going from the compulsiveness of a survivor's comfort zone, wherein we impulsively choose out of fear, into the awareness that we are the creators of the life we desire. As creators, we choose to consciously give ourselves time to be who we authentically want to be.

What I discovered along my journey from compulsiveness to awareness is that compulsive decisions come from the mind, while decisions taken with awareness come from the peaceful space of my true self. It is by getting in touch with our inner self that the most beautiful decisions for our true happiness can be taken. Once we know how to tap into this inner space, we can take the right decisions for our life. We can still enjoy the material, physical aspects of life without getting enslaved to or identified with them.

To do this we have to ask ourselves some tough questions, like: How far do I want to reach? When will it be enough? How much money or safety do I really need to live? It is very important that we ask those questions and find out what is true for us.

At first, these questions scared me. But when I was brave enough to really look at them, I came to the conclusion that I could live nicely with about half of what I had, and that all the rest I was striving for actually wasn't necessary. I realized that I could lower my expectations somewhat, and by doing so, leave myself some precious time to enjoy the things that I really love, like writing, learning new skills, fashion & pattern design, painting, volunteering, reading. I found that I had time left over to simply *be*, instead of *do*. This, in turn, allowed me to give my presence and joy to loved ones and people around me. I gave up making decisions which were against my true self, a habit that I had formed in response to others' expectations or my own fears, which kept me away from realizing what I really wanted.

If you too, have taken or are now taking decisions that are

not based on self-love, I hope that this book will shift your awareness in the right direction and help you change your perspective.

As far as I am concerned, due to my unawareness, I was wandering through life like a car without a navigation system; I didn't take the time to stop, turn inward, read books like this one and realize who I wanted to be. In fact, I remained in a trance-state until life came to wake me up.

I got divorced, which threw me even deeper into my fears, tearing apart everything I had lived for and showing me what *separation* really means. As a consequence, my daughter got sick; I was powerlessly losing her, the soul which is dearest to me. This showed me the true meaning of surrender. My father died of cancer, opening up a battle of love and hate, judgments and forgiveness, teaching me that those dualisms are an illusion. In the process, I learned a lot about compassion. I was then immobilized by a disease for a few months. This taught me that it was high time to learn to love and accept myself radically and to slow down. I had to understand that there was nothing to do and nowhere to go because wherever I am, I am in love with myself. It showed me how to tap into the beautiful essence of my being, which is the only space I need, to be truly happy.

Each of these circumstances caused me to die a bit, and I rose from the ashes with more and more awareness and power until, eventually, I was able to break out of the trance of identity and sculpt the life I truly desired.

I first started taking time for myself, turning inward, and seeking.

But what I was seeking?

At first, I was looking for answers to all of my questions about life, myself and death. Later, I realized that I was really looking for freedom and limitless expression of my creative power and potential. I was seeking to restore my connection with the piece of life that I *am*.

For many years I couldn't find any reasonable answers to my questions. Eventually, I came to understand, that there must not be an intellectual answer to every question. The answers came slowly from within, from my awareness and after a long process. It was not about knowing in an intellectual way; it was more like a longing that drew me towards something I didn't even understand at the time. As I got closer to it, I discovered that what I was longing for was freedom; the freedom from conditioning, attachments, false beliefs about myself, my thoughts, emotions and my illusory identity. This realization brought me quickly and directly to my true self.

I started reading tons of books, travelling to India, and walking the spiritual path, all with the aim of finding answers to my questions. As I did so, I became increasingly confused and thirsty for more. At the end I found that there was nowhere to go and nothing to search for because everything I was looking for was within myself, available to me here and now: the peacefulness, love and beauty of my true essence.

My biggest wish is to help everybody who reads this book to find this space within and merge with it without having to search for a lifetime. May you merge with your true essence and free yourself from the false beliefs about yourself and life. May you transition toward love and self-acceptance for your own being and for all human beings around you. May you move from doing-having-being into being-doing-having, as this is the way life functions. May you transform from passive spectator to creator of the life you desire.

May you open your eyes and realize how beautiful your light is!

Because life is an empty manuscript, you write the story, and the title is: I AM.

The First Myth to Extirpate from your Mind:

Money and external accumulations make my happiness. In my comfort zone, I am happy.

Substitute it with:

Live rather than survive! Your comfort zone is your prison. Break free, nourish your true self and money and success will automatically follow.

1. Decide what is for you, the minimum indispensable to have a safe life.
2. Give yourself time and space to simply *be*, without having to do anything.
3. When you do something, do what matters to you and nobody else but you; completely ignore what others say or think
4. Transform your ambition to get money and power into a vision of creating something that serves your self, human beings and the planet.
5. Move from extracting from people, life, and planet to offering your presence, skills and love, cooperating towards the creation of happy, healthy human beings and a sustainable planet.
6. The way life happens is first *being*, then *doing* and then *having*. Shift into this modus!

HERE IS HOW...

Practices & Tools

Invest Your Time in Creating Your Happiness and the Life You Desire

The first thing we have to become aware of is thoughts like, "I don't have time; when should I do it?" "Who is taking care of my family?" "Is spending so much time turning inward a waste of time?" These excuses go on endlessly, just like when you don't want to do physical activity or sports.

Don't bullshit yourself!

Tell me, is there anything in your life that is more important than you becoming a happy, healthy and realized being? Is it not by being a joyful, free and successful being that your loved ones get the best from you?

We spend five years or more in a university to learn a topic and earn our money, cultivating external wellbeing, so why can't we dedicate some of our time every day for becoming joyful and realized beings, cultivating inner wellbeing?

I suggest that you observe your mind creating excuses to prevent your inner wellbeing. This is just the mind's self-preservation tactic; it knows that when you become happy, you will not need it much anymore.

The truth is that once we have ensured to have enough for our survival, we no longer fear doing more of what nourishes us. Even the thought that spending time on things which don't bring any money could end up being untrue. Many people find that, in the long run, doing what they love turns out to be the most lucrative choice they'll ever make! Beyond this, our success in life comes only when our body, mind and spirit are in alignment. So it is definitely time we start nourishing this graceful space which is our *self*.

The following concrete practices/tools will help you to:

1. Learn to contain the negative thoughts that don't serve you anymore.
2. Discover what you truly love (for all those who, like me, lost touch with it).

1ˢᵗ Practice – Meditation

Your first practice is not to give too much energy to negative thoughts by using meditation. Why meditation? Because sitting silently is the only way to come to that space where you are able to observe your thought patterns and activity with a certain distance, become aware of their madness, and consciously decide to not engage with them. While more complicated techniques are best learned one-on-one with a teacher, this simple meditation is easy to grasp:

1. Integrate meditation in your daily routine. I suggest starting with 12 minutes in the morning and 12 minutes in the evening.
2. Sit silently in a cross-legged posture or in the position most comfortable for you. Keep your spine straight. Place your hands on your legs comfortably, palm downwards. Tilt your head upwards slightly and concentrate on your third eye, or the space between your eyebrows.
3. Breathe slowly in and out, focusing your mind by following the rhythm of your breathing.

4. Let your thoughts be there but don't follow them; simply let them pass without giving them your attention.

5. Observe as your thoughts come and go, becoming aware of their continuous flow. Don't let yourself be dragged into their energy. If this happens, don't resist or make any special effort; simply try to remain in the space of no thoughts.

6. Over time, you will be able to reside in this space for longer and longer. Your thoughts will not stop, as your mind will continue to work, just like your liver, heart and other organs; but eventually you will find that you have ceased to give them attention because they no longer serve you.

7. Don't expect any outcome from meditation. Sit there and *be* in this space without wanting to force, see or feel anything. Simply marinate in the beautiful, lively, silent space you find within.

8. Remember that meditation is not something you do; rather, you become meditative.

Meditation is a great tool to consciously get to know yourself from within. Make use of it and your life will automatically transform for the better. I can assure you this: if it was true for me, it is true for you too, because despite our exterior uniqueness, inside we are all the same!

What If You Still Don't Know What You Want?

If you know exactly what you want, consider yourself lucky. You are a step ahead of most people. The majority of us have lost contact with our self to the extent that we've lost track of our true desires. Some of us desire only from a superficial and unconscious place. We desire what our identity makes us believe we want, and when we get it, we end up disappointed and frustrated.

Happiness is about learning to sense and feel a deeper kind of soul desire, a desire to express our creativity, to share our love, to contribute our best to the world. Only then we are well on our way, as this is where real happiness comes from. Why? Because thought and intention create our reality and if we don't know what we want, it is highly unlikely that the life we desire will manifest. If you have no idea what you want, no idea of your heart's desire, this simple exercise will help:

2ⁿᵈ Practice – Finding the True Qualities of Our Being and What We Really Love

What are the traits and qualities of your true essence? Here's an example of mine:

1. playful
2. generous
3. sensual
4. curious
5. peaceful
6. deep
7. exotic
8. authentic
9. vulnerable
10. graceful
11. artistic
12. principled
13. simple
14. solar
15. energetic

So first, write down at least 20 true qualities of your being. My unique self is……

Now connect to those traits the things that you love to do. Again, we'll use my list as an example:

1. Playful – Dancing, laughing with friends, arts (drawing, coloring), singing
2. Generous – volunteering, giving friends good advice, teaching, coaching
3. Sensual/exotic – traveling to exotic places, listening to Latin and R&B music, loving vibrant, colored fabrics, exotic scents, oils and perfumes
4. Curious – loving books, discovering new things and knowledge, learning new skills
5. Peaceful – loving to walk in nature, looking at a sunset, practicing yoga and meditation

And so on….

Then, start listing potential endings to the following sentence:

If I were not afraid and had enough money, I would…

As you write, be straight and sincere with yourself. Some of my answers were:

1. Change my job for one I love
2. Move near the ocean and nature
3. Create my own fashion collection
4. Marry again (this one made me particularly fearful!)

Then, think back to your childhood and make a list of everything you loved to do as a child. Create some time in your weekly routine to do this activity or to enhance your skills in doing it. If, for example, your activity is painting, try to paint twice a week or book a course for learning painting techniques.

3rd Practice – Write to Get in Touch with Your True Self

Writing is the most effective way to quickly get in touch with our true self. While writing, our intuition is activated and our self reveals answers to questions and everything else we need to know in that moment. Writing is the expression in form of our true essence.

Integrate writing in your daily routine. Find the time to write at least one page every day. It can be about anything: your emotions and thoughts, your questions about different topics or decisions you have to take. Write down everything you can think of. You will see that it will become a great tool to understand your thoughts and emotions, to calm down your fears and reflect realistically about them, and to watch at yourself and your behavior with a bit of distance—the distance you need to learn to be straight with yourself. Writing is a meditative tool that is worth integrating into your lifestyle.

Some people find that writing is not an effective tool for them. If this is your case, choose any other of the tools I've offered here.

4th Practice – Discover Your Needs and Desires

When we first think about what we love and would love to do, a huge number of ideas may come to our mind. In this case it is essential to stay focused and concentrate on the main desires in order not to dissipate our efforts in manifesting too many things at once. This exercise will help you sculpt out your top desires:

First, write down all your needs and desires around these main areas:

a. Body & health
b. Finance
c. Relationships
d. Home
e. Work
f. Creative expression
g. Travel
h. Possessions
i. Spirituality

Formulate your intentions clearly by asking what the most important things you want to manifest out of each area are. Then, out of those intentions, formulate your three main desires.

5th Practice – Make an Action Plan

Now that you have found out what you love and what are the main soul-desires you want to realize most in your life, create an action plan and list all the activities you need to do in order to integrate these desires into your life. These activities could sound like:

- Taking painting lessons.
- Searching for institutions where you could volunteer.
- Improving writing skills.

- Looking for a job more in tune with your true talents and desires.
- Looking for cooperation on a certain topic.
- Adapting a room in your house so it becomes a laboratory for your desired activities.

Done? Perfect! Now create the necessary time to dedicate to your activities without excuses!

My last loving advice for you:

- Always make decisions which reflect love and acceptance for yourself.
- Sculpt a rhythm of life which is ideal for *you.*
- Look for the right job for you and the quantity of time you want to invest in it
- Give yourself a present by allowing enough time to do what truly matters to you.
- Look for a partner who nourishes and supports you, and stay away from "energy vampires"
- Make all your decisions from a place of love for yourself rather than a place of fear (I don't have time; I am not good enough; it is silly to spend time on what I love; I don't deserve it; I don't have enough skills; what will people think, etc.)
- Make your decisions through awareness, never in a compulsive way.

Now, let's look at how to move from compulsiveness to awareness and why it is so fundamental.

Chapter II

FROM COMPULSION TO AWARENESS

"Yesterday I was clever, so I wanted to change the world. Today I am wise, so I am changing myself." - Rumi

Like the breath of life starts with an inhalation at birth and finishes with an exhalation at death, my once joyful, tender little family suddenly stopped breathing. The last exhalation happened as my husband, kneeling down in front of my six-year-old daughter, announced to her that the next day he would leave us.

When I look back on that day from the space of my authentic self, I see beings who were believing their thoughts and giving in to their fears. I can see my story clearly: my little family, so strong and yet fragile, a tiny piece of life within life itself; a little girl, dancing in my arms to the rhythm of a joyful song, the sound and rhythm of life; warm and peaceful beaches, happy get-togethers with family and friends and beautiful safe nights. It was a time full of love and tenderness, which attracted their opposites: harshness and hate. I can see fear and how it powerfully affected all of our decisions and life—all of us, without exception—and yet we were powerless observers, watching at the same scenes again and again, prisoners of the recycled memories and beliefs which keep us trapped and unconscious.

And as everything in the universe expands, transforms in its contrary and, after the maximum moment of expansion, contracts back, my family transformed from gold powder to ash, from love to hate, from joyfulness to suffering.

Despite it all, now that I am in a place of self I know that it was a natural and necessary change and that the drama I lived was all self-created. It was my drama; I suffered from what I thought and believed about myself and others much more than the change itself.

As powerful and sudden as an explosive blast, everything I had lived for and was identified with was shattered by my divorce. My fairytale family life fell apart and I was forced to look into the compulsiveness of my behavior and decisions.

I was completely identified with my marriage. I believed it would last forever. My family and my daughter were everything I lived for to such an extent, that I had completely stopped doing things for myself and creating time and space for my life as a complete and independent being. I lost contact with all my old friends and of course, lost contact to myself.

I was an adaptable child who feared losing the love of my parents if I didn't behave according to their criteria and expectations. Like all adaptable children, I always put great effort into pleasing everybody around me and forcing myself to meet and exceed all their expectations, fearing that if I didn't, I wouldn't be able to survive and be accepted. This was at least the danger degree I felt as a little child.

This exhausting, never-ending effort to be more and more perfect and the fear behind it shaped a distorted identity that had nothing in common with whom I really was.

As a perfectly adaptable child, I continued the same behavioral pattern in my marriage: I constantly made huge efforts to please everybody and make everybody happy apart from me, fearing the loss of their love. This same fear also made me jealous.

Instead of behaving and deciding out of love and awareness, I acted out of fear: the fear of losing loved ones, the fear of rejection. This same fear brought me to destroy other relationships after my marriage. Eventually, it led me to the point where the only thing I wanted was to transcend it and get out from its imprisonment. I was pointing a sharp knife towards myself and stabbing myself little by little. In doing so, I ignored and completely lost track of my self.

As a result, after my divorce, I found myself alone with my daughter, no longer knowing who I was and what I wanted.

Unfortunately, in such situations we are far from being able to remain balanced and aware; instead, the first thing we do is to spontaneously react to the situation emotionally and personally. But guess what? Resisting what is and reacting compulsively to the situation is the worst thing to do, because what we resist will persist—not only that, but it will backfire on us, too. How do I know this? Because this is how I reacted at first.

Since the pain and the grief were too big, I unconsciously suppressed them. I resisted my own emotions and didn't let them find expression, and as a result, I found myself living in resentment, hate and fear. I kept living and struggling like the strong woman I had been educated to be. I didn't want to show my vulnerability and weakness; instead, I kept functioning, because this was the only thing I could do. At least it is what I thought at that time. By disallowing my vulnerability and my emotions, I closed myself in resentment and I became the poor victim who didn't understand why so many ugly things were happening to her.

After some time, I started feeling totally stressed and tired. I felt like I was all alone in this world, with nobody to lend me a hand.

In retrospect, I see that I did not receive any help because I simply did not ask and reach out for it. This is another mistake we often make: We are too full of shame and guilt to look for help. Wanting to deal everything on my own and resisting and suppressing my strong emotions, I became a robot that couldn't notice or feel anything anymore.

I was solving problems, answering ugly lawyer letters, working, earning money and functioning to ensure my daughter's happiness and harmony, so much of which she had lost in the divorce. I felt guilty for what she no longer had. By doing this, I became blind to the true needs and feelings of my daughter and of all those around me. I raised walls of fear, shame, guilt, unworthiness and suffering around me, and they became my impenetrable bastion of defense. Nobody could reach me anymore and I could not reach out.

In a moment of total sadness, I became aware of how I was living—or, better yet, *not* living. This took place nearly two years after my divorce. After bathing in resentment, disease and unhappiness, for those two years, I recognized that I had stopped living; that I was no longer available to myself or to others. Looking at it now, I can see that this sadness was my best friend all along the way because it showed me what I needed to transcend in my life. It was the alarm ringing in my head. When it went off, I realized that I was left with only two choices:

- To continue non-living in a reactive and compulsive mode, not understanding at all where I was heading to, and risk losing my daughter along the way.
- To learn to accept what the situation was, feel the pain of my emotions and assume responsibility for my own happiness.

I finally opted for the second choice, realizing that I had to transcend my fears and compulsions and start living. I stopped resisting my actual life situation and accepted what was.

This wasn't a resigned acceptance or a kind of apathy or lethargy. To the contrary, I started accepting, stopped controlling every situation and other people's behavior, and abandoned myself into the flow of life; by feeling compassionate and loving for myself, I stopped doing and started being. I marinated in the silence and beauty of my being and I consciously took the time to regain my inner balance and clarity. I was a vibrant butterfly but I didn't know it yet; at the time, I was only a caterpillar trying hard to break through.

It was in those silent, long moments with my true essence, in the peaceful and loving space of my being, that I began to make the most conscious and intelligent decisions. By doing so, I was able to take the most effective actions for my true happiness.

This is why it is essential to employ a certain distance as we observe the compulsiveness of our thoughts, behavior and decisions and to consciously decide to slow down. This is awareness. It allows us to become responsible for the best, most joyful output for our inner joy.

With this kind of awareness, we reside in a balanced space— and this allows us to sculpt our life the way we want it.

We can basically perform four types of activities in our life: physical, mental, emotional and energetic. Over the course of the day, how aware are we regarding the activities we perform within those four areas? I'm guessing we're maybe one percent aware, if at all; the rest is unconscious. When we're in this space, it feels like things happen to us almost accidentally.

The more consciously we perform our activities within those four areas, the more control we will gain over our life. If we learn to consciously conduct our life, we can effortlessly shape it the way we want it.

The aim of this book is to give you the tools to enhance your awareness and perception to such a level that you become the creator of your life without needing to undergo too much unnecessary suffering. Though doing this demands a straightforward and sincere look into our compulsive behaviors, it is really worth it!

I had to dismantle all of my illusions and preconceptions about love, relationships, family, life, death and being; I had to lay bare my identity, which was made of opinions, concepts, morality, ego, rights and wrongs, likes and dislikes and discover that they were not me. My identity, my persona is nothing else than my story on this earthly journey; what I am is my true self, an immutable, unshakable, immortal, empty space of pure intelligence and creative energy. This essence is in all of us, and together with our story forms the one being that we are.

If we are aware of the fact that our identity is nothing other than a self-accumulated psychological reality without existential value, and we remain rooted in the power of our true self, we can easily play with our identity in life without identification and attachment to it—and thus without too much suffering. The suffering in life comes when we identify or attach to something or somebody. So only if we completely identify with our identity, we will inevitably suffer, as identity is constantly changing and rooted in the dualism and instability of life.

Once we have realized that we are not it, we are free. We can put on an identity when we need to and drop it when it doesn't serve our happiness. This is what in the Eastern traditions they call *maya*: an illusion, a dream, a state of trance. Through identification with maya, we go through life believing in the distortion of our mental projections—the projections of a self that try to know itself from the outside in. Since the self resides within us, it's no wonder that the way from outside is composed of distortions, duality and separation.

It is when we believe in the distorted projections of our mind that they start having power over us, causing the suffering. The right way to know our self is from the *inside out*. In this way, we are able to see not merely a projection—a reflection—but what we really are. That's why I cannot stress enough the importance of meditation as a powerful mean to learn to perceive things from a distance and merge with our self from within.

Our identity, our story, can only take place because the self exists; the self contains everything which is, and it is from the self that the life-game of the identity pours out. We have to give our energy and attention to our self, not to our identity. The self has to be nourished, listened to and cultivated, because it is the seed from which the fruit of a life anchored in content inner joy springs out. This joy is independent of any external situation.

In order to move from compulsiveness to awareness, it is essential to enhance our perception and the way we "manage" our thoughts, emotions and general response to life. The reactive and compulsive behaviors we adopt in life come from our childhood. We receive unawareness and we learn to respond with unawareness. It seems normal, but it is not.

When I was six, I impulsively punched a window and broke it. My father was trying to help me with homework and I couldn't understand his way of explaining. Of course, what I couldn't see at the time was that he was talking to me from his own fear and sense of insufficiency. If I had then the awareness I have now, the outcome of that situation would have been quite different.

How do we get to this awareness?

At the end of this chapter I will give you a few exercises and tools which will automatically bring you to a higher level of awareness. It is very important to integrate these healthy habits and rituals into your daily routine, as increasing awareness is a constant, regular process. Awareness is not something you own, but what you become.

Can I become aware without using those tools?

Yes, you can become aware, but the process can last more than one lifetime. Not only will it take longer, it will require life itself to bring us more awareness through challenges, which will cost us lots of unnecessary suffering. If we want to reach a certain level of awareness within a short span of time, it is intelligent to make use of the practices and tools that you can find at the end of the chapter.

If we don't do it consciously, life will not let us in peace until we haven't gained the awareness needed in that stage of our evolution. Does this mean life is nasty? No, in reality we are the ones who attract everything that happens to us, because it is exactly what we need in order to be pitchforked into the next level of awareness and into the next evolution cycle.

It is life and we are life. We create our own playground and use it to enhance our awareness as human beings. The best way to handle this is to get out of challenging situations transformed and smarter—instead of hurt and wounded.

I would definitely not be the person I am today without all the suffering and the sadness I experienced during my life. The compassion, understanding and love for others and ourselves can only be learned through all life situations when we decide to take responsibility for our happiness and our own life, rather than getting beat up and becoming lethargic victims.

The junction is always between:

- Self-love, radical acceptance of ourselves, awareness, life and
- Self-hate, blame, guilt, stagnancy, unconscious suffering, death.

Our journey is the journey through our own beings and toward our true self. Once we discover it and merge with it, the true life-journey can begin.

Second Myth to extirpate from your mind:

I am a victim, I don't understand why all this is happening only to me, I have not done anything bad to attract all this ugliness.

Substitute it with:

I am aware that what I attract is exactly what I need to better understand my true self and reach a higher level of consciousness.

I am aware that the choices I make today will affect the quality of life I have tomorrow. I am aware that I am the creator of my life and not a passive spectator of it.

1. Look straight into yourself.
2. Seek for the cyclical mental and emotional patterns that don't serve you.

3. Become aware of them.
4. Develop Self-Love and radical acceptance for yourself.
5. Increase your awareness and the way you perceive people and situations.
6. You are the one who decides if a situation or person will bring you joy or sadness.
7. You are the sculptor of your life!

HERE IS HOW...

Practices & Tools

Ayurvedic Daily Routine

The first thing we need to do to increase our awareness and perception about us, life and the people around us, is to create silent time in our daily routine. To do so, we'll employ remedies from ayurveda, an alternative method for health and wellbeing that has been practiced in India for over 5000 years. This system of knowledge comes from ancient India. In Sanskrit, the word *ayurveda* means "science of life." It teaches us that we are microcosms, universes within ourselves. Ayurveda is based on the idea that every human being is capable of self-healing.

There is no way we can bring light onto everything unconscious within us if we are frenetically functioning all the time.

Yes, you understood me right. No excuses and no exceptions! It is impossible to increase our level of awareness if we are constantly busy, running from point A to point B and never living in the moment. So, the first thing is to adjust your daily routine to a pace that allows you enough time to take care of your inner balance and increase your awareness.

Second, we spend lot of time talking and talking; in order to enhance perception and awareness, we have to spend the same amount of energy on perception that we spend on expression. Ayurvedic science suggests that a routine and some healthy rituals are essential for the balance and alignment of body, mind and spirit, which is self.

Below, I've provided an adjusted excerpt out of a typical Ayurvedic daily routine which will allow you to create the necessary space and the healthy conditions to get in touch with your true self in different little moments during the day. To start, I suggest that you take only the bits and pieces that work for you and apply them in your life.

- **Wake Up Before Sunrise**

This is very important so that you can synchronize with the rhythm of the sun and live within the natural cycles. Waking up at this time was very natural for our ancestors, who knew how to live following life's natural rhythm. This healthy habit was increasingly lost in modern society, and this is one of the reasons our minds are so mis-aligned. Just before sunrise, a great shift in energy fills the atmosphere and the environment is pure, calm and soothing; this is considered the best time for meditation, as the mind can clear more easily. Look online to see when the sun rises in your area and get up at least half an hour ahead of time.

- **Practice Hatha Yoga in the Morning**

Hatha yoga *asanas* are from the Sanskrit for "sit down." Commonly known as yoga postures, they're actually designed to help us meditate more easily. If regularly practiced, they can align body, mind and energies, leading to better health, deeper awareness and concentration. One specific sequence of asanas is known as the sun salutation. Asanas are frequently accompanied by *pranayama*, or breath exercises.

How much and what exactly you practice is up to you; you

can do a few asanas or the sun salutation, some pranayama, a sitting meditation, or a combination of all of the above.

At the beginning, I suggest that you insert only one of the practices into your morning routine, and over time, as you get used to the exercises, you will be able to add some more.

- **Time Your Meals Appropriately**

Suggested Ayurvedic mealtimes for keeping good health are: breakfast before 8:00 AM, lunch around 12:00 PM, dinner at 6:00 PM at the latest. This allows enough time for proper digestion between meals and before sleeping.

- **Focus on Your Food**

Make a habit of eating slowly in silence and being conscious of what you eat, the water you drink and the air you breathe. Base your diet on fruits, vegetables and legumes, food that is nearer to nature and that your body can digest without too much effort. Take the time to think about how many people contributed to the meal you are eating and thank them for it. Gratitude is a great tool to increase awareness. In this way, before eating, we choose consciously how we want to respond to our food. If we have this conscious response to food, our food will also behave well within our body.

- **Walk After Lunch**

This is a great way to disconnect from work stress and get

in contact with the silent space within us. Even if for only a few minutes, walking is a natural meditation. Walk with awareness of animals, things and persons around you. Try not to engage with your mind as you walk.

- **Practice Hatha Yoga Just Before Sunset**

How much and what exactly you practice is up to you; you can do a few asanas or the sun salutation, some pranayama, a sitting meditation, or a combination of all of the above.

At the beginning I suggest you to insert only one of the practices in your morning routine. Grow that practice first. Then, as this becomes habit, you will be able to add another practice in the evening.

If the evening yoga is too much for you, try to sit in silence for at least 12 minutes without giving attention to your thoughts.

If you prefer to go to gym or run after work, you can skip the evening yoga session completely.

- **Go to Bed Around 10:00 PM**

It is very important not to check your email or do work right before going to sleep. This time should be dedicated to art, music, writing, spiritual teachings, and everything which enhances perception and awareness; it induces us to calmness of mind and spirit and prepares us for a healthy sleep.

This revised version of an ayurvedic daily routine is an effective one that is not too difficult to integrate in your daily life. Nevertheless, it is not meant to stress your life even further, so please make sure that you adapt it to your needs.

Pay Attention to Everything

In order to enhance awareness, it is essential to increase our level of perception. Most of us are constantly living in our own psychological reality to the point that we are rarely in the present moment. By always dwelling in the past or future, we walk through life without paying attention to almost anything.

Has it ever occurred to you when talking with a colleague or a neighbor that you are already thinking about the next answer you will give? Or, have you caught yourself developing a mental judgment about someone while you are speaking to them?

When is the last time you were present, observing the sunset or the moon?

Have you ever paid attention to the patterns of a leaf or the colors of a bird?

Don't worry, this happens to almost all of us. This is the price we pay for having to live in the frenetic rhythm of the modern society.

In order to learn to sense our true essence, which is no-form, it is essential to enhance our perception and sensitivity. The most direct way to do this is to pay absolute attention to everything.

Next time you will go for a walk in nature, take your time stop and attentively observe a tree or a leaf, a crawling creature, or simply try to read beyond a person who passes by. Shut down your intellect and don't try to name, dissect or judge the object of your observation. Simply be with it and see what happens. If you are worried that people will think you are crazy, choose a place and a moment where you are alone.

By training your sense organs to look deeply and sensitively at things, people and nature, you are unconsciously widening your awareness.

For people who love art, it can be fun to look around and search for themes to be used later on for our art. For example, I love pattern design and no matter where I am, whether it's nature, in an airport, or a local marketplace, I pay attention to original patterns and draw them on a book I always take with me, or I take pictures of them to use them for inspiration later. The huge palette of creativity nature and common things can contain is unbelievable!

We don't need to force ourselves to perceive things, people or nature. In a natural way, if we put our intention toward it, the result will manifest spontaneously. When we learn to look at everything with deep attention we will notice a great shift in the quality of our exchange with people, nature and other creatures.

As you can see, willingness and responsibility are the only things you need to increase your level of awareness and live a physically and mentally healthy life. Become responsible for your happiness and wellbeing by consciously choosing new healthy habits!

Chapter III

THE IMPORTANCE OF ASSUMING RESPONSIBILITY

"If you are irritated by every rub, how will your mirror be polished?" - Rumi

I was barely divorced and emotionally lost, alone with a six-year-old girl to whom I could not explain what had happened because I did not yet understand it myself. Overwhelmed by my compulsive emotions, I felt like a shaky little wooden boat in the middle of a vortex on a stormy ocean. Not knowing how to react to this situation, I decided to act as if nothing had happened, suppressing my feelings and continuing to merely function. I chose to blame and resent others and hate myself for my own decisions that had led me to where I stood.

I was not awake enough to choose responsibility for myself and my life; instead, I gave the responsibility for my happiness over to everybody else and lost other important years in unhappiness.

While everybody around me was building a new life, trying to become happy again, I was pouring myself into a self-made soup full of my apparent enemies, inhuman injustices, guilt, shame, misery and hate. It's no wonder that I got so poisoned by that soup, the soup of my mind, which I fully believed to be true.

When I discovered later that nothing could have been further from the truth than my self-created psychological reality, I understood that my time had come to accept full responsibility for my own happiness; that nobody was going to give it to me from the outside and that it was my responsibility to make myself into a joyful being from within, somebody who doesn't need to extract anything from others to be happy, but who is full of love and happiness within and a gift for everybody around; a being who is conscious of her own beautiful light and can be the soul of every place at any given moment.

The turning point came when I realized—not only on an intellectual level, but in an experiential way—that I, and I only, am responsible for my happiness and that it's my job to make myself into the being I want to have around me. It may sound simple, but it takes a lot of willingness to not bullshit ourselves and to take a straight, sincere look inside of us and realize this. To do so, it is essential that we overcome the negative power of the mind, learn to contain it and completely drop our identification with it if we want to get there.

We are the only ones responsible for who we are and for our happiness.

Now that I have explained what responsibility means, let's underline what taking responsibility *doesn't* mean:

1. Forcing yourself to always help others.
2. Forcing yourself to always be a "good" person.
3. Taking a larger workload than you can properly manage.
4. Being the one who always feels bound to solve a conflict first.

5. Staying with a partner that is not nourishing for you and your evolution.

It is essential to underline that responsibility has a lot to do with radical love and acceptance for yourself. Only somebody who has discovered the beauty of his/her own authentic self can assume responsibility in a healthy way. The two simply go together.

How can we take responsibility for our own happiness in a healthy way?

It starts with becoming aware of how to respond to any given situation in any given moment. This requires us to have the right inner balance—which comes from our perception, our awareness—to respond to a situation by consciously choosing our thoughts and emotions. It also requires us to be able to think about possible consequences before they become a reality.

Most of the time, we don't; we give responsibility over to the other and we compulsively respond by giving five-star treatment to our outmost ugly thoughts about ourselves and others. We follow our cyclical mental patterns, triggered by past memories and emotions—the so-called *pain-body*—and burst out, displaying the worst of us, which we mostly will later regret.

It is important to understand that the other person is not responsible for our reaction—we are. The old memories and emotions are stored and lie latent inside of us; it is our responsibility to see them, accept them and let them pass so that they will not keep affecting our relationships with others.

We cannot be a slave to everyone outside of us who consciously or unconsciously triggers our pain-body; it is our responsibility to find and release the emotions stored within us; it is our responsibility to learn not to take everything personally so we can feel untouched and happy, no matter what the others say or do.

Unfortunately, for millions of years, human beings have been following their cyclical thought patterns, releasing the ugliest reactions and hurting themselves and others. It is time, here and now, to realize that we are the creators of our suffering. If we take a close look, only a small percentage of human suffering is caused by outside circumstances; the rest is caused by the emotional and psychological response coming from within us. It is not the situation itself but our emotions and thoughts about it that make us suffer.

Our belief and our identification with our emotions and our thought process cause most of our suffering, and we are one hundred percent responsible for it! It means we have the power to break our beliefs and the identification with our mind; we have the power to become the sculptor of our life and destiny.

Let's take our anger as an example. We become angry not because somebody said or did something, but because we took it personally; we filtered what this person said or did through our interior world made of memories, beliefs, opinions and judgments, then we project our distorted view without being aware of the consequences. Everything we perceive comes from within us.

If other people's behavior can decide whether our day will be joyful or miserable, we are surely not free beings, but real slaves of external people and circumstances. Taking responsibility for our inner harmony and happiness makes us free!

When two partners are fighting, they always both think they are right—sound familiar?

When this happens, we can either break up the relationship because neither of the partners is aware enough to respond behind the right or wrong scheme, or we can preserve the relationship by choosing which end to this fight-story we wish for ourselves and respond consciously to get there. We can only be capable of the latter response if we have gone beyond our identification with our thought process and our emotions. This requires us to shed a bit of our ego and identity.

Is the capability to shape every situation of our life exactly as we want it not comparable to the power of a creator?

Alternatively, we can continue to allow every situation and person to ruin our inner harmony. But if we could consciously choose between the two options, which one would we choose?

When I talk about the mind, I am always asked the following questions:

Why is the mind so ugly? Why does it want to bring us suffering?

The mind is not ugly; it is only doing its job, which is to preserve our safety and our survival. The problem is that it cannot understand when its alarm is truly needed (e.g. in the case of physical survival) or and when it is not (e.g. in human relationships), so it ends up sounding this alarm all the time. In relationships, for example, it is not about striving for physical survival but about looking for understanding.

So, when we fight with somebody, it will sound the alarm by creating a myriad of reasons why the other is ugly and we are not, and why we should fight him/her. If we believe those thoughts, we will act compulsively, but if we question them calmly, we will find out that they are based on false beliefs we have about ourselves, which the mind triggers us to "defend".

The question is, why should we let the mind defend beliefs that don't serve us, our happiness or our life?

Here is where it comes to our pure intelligence and the capacity to see things without identifying with them.

Every time we find ourselves wanting to be right, resisting, re-acting, controlling what is, making other people bad, or feeling too proud to give in, we are residing in our identity.

This leads us to separate from ourselves and the other, which inevitably brings suffering. With awareness, we can observe the situation with enough distance to realize the truth about ourselves and other people and opt for a different outcome. This can save us from a lot of wasted energy, confusion and suffering in our relationships.

There is no right or wrong way to respond to situations; no morality or judgment needs to be involved. We only have to be sure that our behavior doesn't lead us to suffer the consequences afterwards. If we can live happily with the consequence, it is fine.

If we love harmony, let's create more of it. Why talk about world peace if we are not able to be peacefully with ourselves and with those around us?

We need to understand that the people around us are not the trash bin for our mind and our unresolved childhood issues. We are responsible for making ourselves happy and balanced beings who can create harmony and joy in our own lives and the lives of those around us. We can start by scratching the mud from the window of our eyes—otherwise we will always see dirt in others. I say this because most of the time, the negative things we see in others are nothing else than the dirt of our own unresolved issues projected onto them. If we get angry, it is not because of the other person but because we didn't look and transform our past anger. Unresolved, our anger remains stored there, waiting for somebody or something to trigger it.

Sometimes it can be hard for us to look with neutrality at the truth, but it is only by looking at the truth without fear and accepting what is that we will reach freedom and inner peace. It will lead us to a totally different quality of life and will also enhance the quality of the relationships with others.

Despite the fact that what we face in life situations is

sometimes ugly, it's important that we see it, because it is often a sense of guilt and shame about this ugliness that causes us to look inward. Once we look, we find out that we were children subjected to the unawareness of others, but that this is not an excuse to keep spreading unawareness. The unawareness that caused and keeps causing us great pain can always be transformed into compassion and love for ourselves. Every day, we have a chance to use each little life situation into a chance for transformation. If we avoid looking at our past pains and hurt, we are damned to perpetuate unawareness.

That is why is essential to look into the roots of our pain from childhood and past, feel the powerlessness, and transform it into awareness, love and compassion. These characteristics keep us true to our original self and facilitate connection with ourselves and other people. Running away only perpetuates pain and suffering for ourselves and for others.

The process of self-transformation is the most beautiful act of love that we can do for the people we love and for all the others on this planet who are making the same journey.

To be clear, I am not suggesting that we "fix" ourselves; we are already perfect and whole in the authenticity of our true divine nature. Self-transformation needs to be done without judgment involved; everybody acts in a given situation according to their stage of awareness. There's no use in beating ourselves up for not having a higher level of awareness at a certain point in time in the past. After all, we're in a learning process. This is the way it is meant to be so that we can evolve further. Life offers us situations, and we have the free will to choose between one behavior or the other. What we choose indicates our state of awareness.

It is time to stop criticizing ourselves and others and to start to look with sincerity and love within ourselves. We have to look inside with love and compassion, just as a mother has for the child who is learning.

And we can extend that love and compassion to others, too. After all, we cannot change anybody; this is not our job, especially when the person is not ready for change or transformation. We can only evolve ourselves into more and more aware beings. By doing so, we become an example and inspiration for others, and when they are ready, they will open to awareness and light. There is no criticism, judgment or morality involved in this process.

Third Myth to extirpate from your mind:

Situations or people outside are responsible for my compulsive response to life and for my negative emotions (anger, jealousy, hate, resentment, etc.). I can't take self-responsibility because that will mean I will always have to help and understand everybody, leading me to be misused and misunderstood.

Substitute it with:

I am 100% responsible for the way I respond to a situation, including my thoughts, my emotions and my reactions. If I take responsibility, I learn to better know and manage my thoughts and emotion; I become the sculptor of the life I want and I am completely free from opinions, judgments and the behavior of other people. I can consciously choose when to help, respecting my own boundaries and limits. I see people and situations in a neutral way, without the filter of my identity, and can detach from critics and personal resentments. I learn to understand and respect myself and others.

- Be straight and sincere to yourself
- Know yourself; learn to neutrally look at your morality, opinions, prejudices, thoughts and emotions—including the ugliest ones.
- Look without judgment, criticism or self-hate but with love, compassion and patience.
- The more you learn to see, the more you are aware, the more you are freed of your own compulsions and ego and from other people's opinions and judgments.
- Being responsible doesn't mean having to act all the time; it can be only the way you respond to a situation. If somebody is having a problem, you don't necessarily have to find time and help. You can simply support with words, or simply with a smile; the most important thing is that you have *something* to offer.
- Transform yourself from the actor to the creator of your life.

May you learn to take responsibility and understand the fears, false beliefs and prejudices that force you to live imprisoned in your own compulsive, cyclical mental and emotional patterns—patterns which no longer serve you.

May you break out of this prison of unawareness and spread your wings toward the unlimited possibilities at your disposal to shape your life.

The place is HERE. The time is NOW.

And always remember:

**"The world is full of nice people. If you
don't find one, be one." – Rumi**

HERE IS HOW...

Practices & Tools

Finding Your Responsibility

Look straight into yourself, complete the following sentences and add what you want to do differently from now on. Remember that it is not about taking responsibility as identity but about finding out what will lead to your true happiness.

Keep completing them even if irritation arises. If you want to add some more, feel free to do so, remembering to end each sentence with a positive intention:

I am responsible for..........
I am responsible for..........
I am responsible for..........
I am responsible for..........
I am responsible for..........
I am responsible for..........
I am responsible for..........

For example:

- I am responsible for my toxic thoughts and emotions, for allowing them to pollute my mind and making me and others feel bad. Instead, I am not giving them energy so that they can quickly dissolve. I use them to understand their roots and transform them into positive energy.
- I am responsible for all the unhappy relationships that I created for myself. Instead, I love and accept myself radically, so that I attract only loving relationships. I understand that I cannot own anybody and that what I

try to control and manipulate will run away, while what I am, will attract the same.

- I am responsible for consciously or unconsciously needing other people to appreciate me, comfort me and respect me, as if that would make me a complete, whole being. Instead, I take care of my transformation and learn to appreciate, comfort and respect me. Also, I know my value and my true nature.

- I am responsible for the accusations, criticisms and judgments that I make toward others and myself which, like swords, cut the wings of my Spirit and the Spirit of other beings. Instead, I consciously learn to use gentle words, or at least words that don't hurt the core of a person. If I am not capable of this, I choose to be silent.

Enjoy doing the practices and try to avoid self-criticism as you do them. They are meant to dissipate the fog that keeps your true self and essence in the shadow.

Keep rubbing at your skin (identity) until it becomes so thin that you can perceive that which is within you (self).

Chapter IV

HEAVEN IS A STATE OF MIND: MIND & CO.

"One of the marvels of the world: The sight of a soul sitting in prison with the key in its hand."- Rumi

In times of great strife, I wrote the following in my journal:

".......yes, I am happy! But why am I so scared to admit it? Maybe because I already know that sadness will follow. Part of myself is afraid of being happy. Why do I fear my own happiness? Because I don't think I deserve it? Because of all the mistakes I did? .... Why is it so damned difficult for me to understand myself, love myself and realize who I really am and what I truly love?..."

"Have I adapted myself too much in this relationship? Is it wrong to get happiness from making others happy? Or is it only wrong, to crop my wings to make others happy?..."

"I am unhappy because today I became aware that I cannot tie the people I love to me; nothing and nobody belongs to me and I don't belong anybody. But why does the awareness of that, hurt so much? Am I unhappy because I fear to lose him, or because in reality I could never and I will never be able to bind him? Why do I need to bind him, after all?"

"I am tired; my thoughts travel at the speed of light through all the things I have to do. Why am I not able to substitute what I think I must do with what I love to do? And what is that I really love to do? If I only knew it for sure…It is so frustrating that I have lost myself to the extent that I not even know what I truly love anymore. I can't find true meaning in anything anymore."

"It's easy for them to say: love yourself! But what does this concretely mean? What is it that I have to do? I always thought that I love myself; if so, why do I criticize and beat myself up so much? What is that I cannot accept? What is it that I don't want to see and feel? What exactly am I escaping from? The pain of ignorance, or the stupidity of my false beliefs?"

At the time, I was on the journey toward discovering my true self and desperately searching for answers.

Do these thoughts sound somehow familiar to you? Are my doubts, fears, and uncertainties not common in all of us?

The thoughts that have kept humanity trapped for millions of years are always the same and are based on the same false beliefs we have of ourselves: inadequacy, self-hatred, rejection, guilt and shame, denial of who we are.

The fact that we think our false beliefs are true creates a myriad of negative thoughts that bring up fear. Such beliefs and thoughts kept me imprisoned for many years; I believed I am my mind and I was completely identified with it; I gave my thoughts my undivided attention, scaring myself with the fears that came from them, until I was able to observe and break this cyclical game.

In this chapter, we'll take a look at how I did that. It is time to break the spell and see the play of our mind, exploring our total identification with thoughts and emotions.

Mind, Thoughts and Emotions

The mind is a very powerful instrument that underwent millions of years of evolution to reach its state of development. Because of our thought-capacity, we are able to create all the technologies we need for survival, material wealth and comfort in life. At the same time, the mind can become a cutting knife when it starts to control us. Are we thinking or are our thoughts thinking us?

As far as I am concerned, I could clearly observe that when my thoughts took over, they violently drew me into the future and the past, taking me away from the beauty and the peace of residing in the moment and in contact with my true self. My mind was in control and I thought I could never stop all those thoughts—but it turned out that this was also only a thought! I learned that if I stopped believing in the thoughts that didn't serve me, they visited me less and less often. By believing and giving all my energy to those thoughts, I was perpetuating them. Thoughts are like parasites; they can only survive if they find the right terrain in which to flourish.

I learned that it wasn't about warring with or start hating my thoughts—this just made them stronger. Instead, I figured out how to silently observe them and consciously stop giving them my attention. I found that humor was a great way to get rid of their drama; it is the best antidote against negative thoughts, because as soon as we stop giving them energy and attention, they can no longer exist. We created our thoughts, and it is in our power to contain them by taking over leadership. As you see, good leadership starts inside of us!

It is so beautiful to reside in the calmness and intelligence of our true self; it is to be found always in the here and now, never in the past or future. Don't let the psychological, illusory reality which your mind creates become your prison and set illusory limitations to the evolution of your being and your life. Your true power is to simply be in the moment, because it is there that you enter the intelligent, powerful space which is your true essence, your true self. This is not a space of inactivity and inertia. To the contrary, this is the space where all your best ideas and actions come from.

I was once very confused. Thoughts about the past and future overwhelmed me and my mind was in complete turmoil. I remember reaching for a pen, asking in desperation: "How do I get to merge with my true self and reside there? When will I be free of all of those unnecessary thoughts? When is it my time to merge with the beauty and peace of the now? When will I stop being in fear of those ugly thoughts?"

After a while, I dried my tears and found myself writing:

The distance between you and your true self is composed of your own thoughts and your engagement with them.

In that moment I understood that my own questions came out of my engagement with my thoughts and the belief I had in them. I thought it was impossible for me to free myself from what I thought of as my thought-diarrhea. By believing in those thoughts, I was creating the reality that I would never get there. Desperation followed.

It is as easy as that—and also so difficult. But I am the living proof that is not impossible!

We are not our mind; our mind only belongs to us. Why believe we are a drop of water when in reality, we are the entire ocean?

It is when I understood this, not only conceptually but as a life experience, that I started taking the best decisions for my life and future and living magically with freedom, happiness and wellbeing.

It is my wish and my blessing that you get in touch with your pure essence, an intelligence free from the influence of old memories and thought-patterns. We are all unique in the external expressions of our potential, but the basic pure intelligence within is the same for all of us.

If I was able to dissociate from my mind and become free and constantly in touch with my true self, each of you can do it too!

Remember: The distance between you and your true self is composed of your own thoughts.

Let's have a closer look at the mind.

The content of the mind is not our choice; the mind is an accumulation of memories, impressions, beliefs, philosophies, notions, and opinions accumulated during a lifetime through education, religion, media, etc.

Everything we have come in touch with over the course of our life has been absorbed by the mind and is stored within it. We can compare the mind to a big trash bin; on one side, it is useful, like a trash bin in a house, but on the other side, if we think that the trash bin is greater than the house and start sleeping in it and identifying with it, this is a big problem.

The mind is a fantastic instrument if it is used when it's needed and kept silent when it's not. Unfortunately, today our mind is constantly working and "thinking" us. Nearly everybody has this dis-ease; it is kind of socially accepted. That is why I put so much weight on the mind. I want us to see and understand that it is not healthy for us to inhabit the mind to the extent that it becomes like a true reality for us. We don't want to live in the conditioned reality of the mind.

By observing my mind with distance, I found out that it follows a certain pattern:

1. We create a thought; for example: I can't make it.
2. We give this thought importance and energy. We identify with it and believe that we are inadequate, insufficient, "not enough."
3. The identification with the thought, connected with past memories creates emotions such as sadness, sense of inadequacy and depression.
4. The emotion is felt as real, instead of being seen as a projection of our mind created out of recycled past memories.

This is a vicious circle of unnecessary negative emotions and suffering. Once we believe the thought, it's no wonder that we develop fears, depression and mental stress.

How to break this vicious circle?

1. We learn to observe our mind patterns and strategy creating a little distance between us and the mind. Meditation is an excellent way to do this.
2. We learn to question the validity of our thoughts.

Heaven is a state of mind and you can create it for yourself!

Fourth Myth to extirpate from your mind:

I am my body and my mind.

Or, in Descartes' more familiar terms: "Cogito ergo sum" (I think, therefore I am).

Substitute it with:

I am not my body. I am not my mind. My body is an accumulation of food. My mind is an accumulation of impressions from outside; my mind, like my body, belongs to me but it is not me. I am the self, a space of pure intelligence and awareness, love, peace and beauty. I am simply being-ness/existence/life. I don't live. I am life.

I am not because I think. But because I am, I can think.

- Just like we get diarrhea from eating the wrong food, we get mental diarrhea by dwelling in negative/unnecessary thoughts.
- We are not our minds and our bodies; instead they are instruments at our disposal to create a life of joy, peace and balance.
- Only if we observe the mind from outside can we get the right balance to consciously decide how to behave in any given situation.
- We don't have to identify with anything we are not, but be capable of making use of what is ours (mind and body) without identification.
- Just like we control how to use our hands, we have to learn how to contain our mind and thoughts; we don't want our most important faculty to be out of our control.

HERE IS HOW...

Practices & Tools

Yoga, Meditation and Self-Inquiry

1st. practice – Practice Yoga

There are specific yoga postures which, if done properly, can perfectly prepare you for more powerful meditation techniques. These postures must be done with a high level of perfection and very slowly. Mastering them will make sure that your body, mind and energies are aligned and this will create the perfect conditions to take with you in your meditation.

I suggest that you learn those postures only in specific yoga centers, because when poorly taught, yoga can be extremely counter-productive for your body and health.

You can send me an email at the address at the end of this book and I will be glad to forward you to the right Yoga centers in your city/country.

2nd. Practice - Meditation (next level)

Learning to observe your own thoughts works only if you create a space between you and your mind. Therefore, I advise you, *again*, to use meditation!

There are very simple, but extremely effective meditations, which are a combination of breathing techniques, chanting and silent meditation in one.

It will take about twenty minutes every day and you will notice results very soon. It means you will be able to observe your own mind patterns, increase your awareness, and with the time, the noise in your mind will automatically slow down. Like the Yoga postures, these kinds of meditations need to be transferred properly and cannot be taught through a book. I promise you that investing your time into learning such a powerful meditation is really worth it!

Meditation is simply being; there is nothing to do during meditation. Rather, here's what *not* to do:

- Don't try to stop or repress your thoughts and emotions; this is the best way to increase them, and we don't want that!
- Don't engage with your thoughts. Thoughts will appear during meditation; just like your liver, heart and kidneys, your mind will keep working. This is normal. Simply don't follow them and don't give them energy and attention
- Don't expect to see images or voices. Shut down your imagination and senses. There is nothing to see or listen to there; there is a silent, loving space to merge with.
- Don't make any effort of any kind. Drop your expectations out of the meditation, drop the things you must do, who you have to be, how good you have to become; drop all judgments and opinions about yourself. In one sentence: stop doing and awaiting, and simply be in silence.

Enjoy your meditation! Once you have experienced your true essence, even if only for a few minutes, you will understand the importance of it. My meditation time slots are the most loved in my daily routine today. I long to spend this beautiful time with my self, where I get to experience the joy of abiding in the love and beauty of my essence.

3rd. Practice – Self-Inquiry

As far as questioning your thoughts is concerned, I highly recommend Byron Katie's method, "The Work." This is the most powerful method for self-inquiry and will awaken you from the dream of believing your thoughts and false beliefs about yourself. Find out more at www.thework.com

If you find it too difficult to apply the method to your personal situation, you can contact a facilitator from Byron Katie's website or book one of the Inner Management workshops on my website; in all the workshops I offer, we dedicate a big part to "The Mind & Co." and we help people with self-inquiry using several other methods, taking practical life examples as a basis.

The only thing you need to take with you is the bravery, willingness, openness and sincerity to find the truth about yourself.

Dissociating from your own thoughts when they don't serve you, is your responsibility and the only way to achieve a free and joyful life. You will make peace with yourself and consequently with the entire world.

Stepping out of your thoughts means living in the present moment, and the present moment is always perfectly fine. Life is made of many present moments, and they are always perfectly fine—as long as your thoughts don't put a shadow on everything.

You can make it, no matter how tough it may seem at the beginning. If I did it, you can do it too! And so it is.

Chapter V

ENTANGLEMENT: MY BIGGEST CHALLENGE

"Your task is not to seek for love, but merely to seek and find all the barriers within yourself that you have built against it." - Rumi

Let's get it straight: We are identified with almost everything we come in contact with during the course of our life. We are identified with our jobs, wives/husbands, children, money, bodies, minds, thoughts, emotions, nationality, religions…the list goes on and on.

At the basis of our identification, there are false beliefs about ourselves that make us feel incomplete and insufficient. This sense of inadequacy makes us needy, always in search of something or somebody to identify with and attach to. This is why many of us are attached to people, behaviors, roles, opinions, organizations, religions and much, much more.

The false beliefs about ourselves are deeply rooted within us and have been accumulated throughout our childhood. They then keep perpetuating themselves throughout the course of our life.

From the moment we come to life, our authentic self has been bombarded by teachings, doctrines, emotional threats, more or less humiliating judgments, wrong advice and moral rules, which have completely conditioned and overwhelmed us to the point that we have lost sight, of who we really are.

Our being has undergone a sort of brainwashing from all kinds of people: parents, teachers, religious preachers and media. To be very frank, the parents and teachers who were unhappy and unrealized in their life taught us that their way of thinking, emoting and living was the right one for us! People and institutions keep making us believe that what didn't work for them is what will make our happiness. Why? And why do we keep perpetuating this modus?

Many parents keep pushing (more or less unconsciously) their children to study something only for the sake of money, even when working only for the sake of money, suppressing their true talents and passions, made them unhappy, unrealized and frustrated human beings.

As we have been totally conditioned, we couldn't help building up a false identity of who we are (the manager, good person, sexually okay, Roman Catholic, money-dedicated), believing this is us, and defending this identity to gain acceptance in society. Basically, we have come to believe that who we truly are must be wrong, incomplete and insufficient. This is the origin of the first huge false belief about ourselves: The way we are is not good enough. It's no wonder that many more false beliefs followed.

I am, like most of us, one of these beings. I believed for much of my life that there must be something insufficient and wrong with me. When I was a child, no matter how well I did at school or sports, they were never good enough—or, in the rare circumstances that they were good enough, I took them for granted. I don't blame my parents for this; I take full responsibility for feeling this way. This was my own creation. My parents only did what they believed to be right at that time, with their level of awareness—just as each of us is doing with our own children. I am talking about my childhood merely to explain how the false beliefs we have about ourselves start creating themselves during childhood and are responsible for shaping our future identity.

Over time, I came to understand that whenever others put me down in any way, their actions and words are only the projections of their own state of pain and confusion. Their put-downs were nothing more than their reaction to the false beliefs they have about themselves. In the same way, my perceptions can also be only the projections of my own beliefs and the pain coming from them.

Growing up as a woman in a Catholic and patriarchal country was very difficult for me. I had to give a lot and received little acceptance and credit in return. It's no wonder that I started thinking that there must have been something basically wrong with me and that huge effort was needed. This false belief was anchored within myself and accompanied me for many years.

Believing that I was wrong and somehow insufficient, I started doing and being all sorts of things to desperately gain attention, admiration and acceptance—unconsciously, of course—and drifting away from my authentic self. This pattern perpetuated throughout most of my life.

When we believe we are wrong, we spend all of our life avoiding rejection. How does this work? Behaving in such a needy, dependent, controlling, fearful way leads us to attract exactly what we don't want: rejection! I did this for many years with my relationships; my fear of being rejected attracted men who were fearful and, most of all, unconscious themselves.

This is the way universe works: what we fear and think creates vibrations that create our reality. Once I started becoming aware of my thoughts and emotions and questioning the beliefs about myself, I realized that I had always been clearly loved by my family—in fact, they taught me many positive, important values and were always there for me. I understood that it was only their degree of awareness that led them to create certain behaviors that I took in as unloving. Their behavior was not personal; rather, it was only the result of their compulsive, unaware reaction to a situation.

As I started to notice that I was behaving in a compulsive, unaware way with my daughter, I understood that this is the only way we can learn and grow. Once we truly see ourselves, it is easy to learn to be compassionate, patient and understanding to ourselves, as we see that we can only do our best with the awareness that we have. In the same way, we can learn to see our parents and others people through the eyes of compassion. As a consequence, all of the resentment, hate, judgments and negative emotions that we once stored within just vanish.

It is essential to be to ourselves, just as we wished our parents would have been with us. It's important to embrace ourselves with the same unconditional love and patience that a mother has for her own child. By learning to love our imperfections and our past errors, we learn to forgive ourselves and, consequently, all those that we have been blaming for our misery.

But in reality, there is nothing to forgive because we all do the best we can with the degree of awareness that we have at a given point in time in our evolutionary growth. We can't act in any other way. So why do we feel guilty in the first place?

Similarly, we all try to defend our identity in order to become happy. This is our human nature. All of us are trying to be happy in different ways. So most of the time that a person seems to be against us on a personal level, they are not.

We only feel this way because we are trapped in the illusory reality of our identity—our mind, thoughts and emotions. Once our awareness reaches a certain level, we are able to see through different eyes and transcend our recycled thought-patterns and emotions. We can see through our false beliefs and understand that we create this personal drama all by ourselves. From there, switching to the understanding that we create our own happiness is not so difficult. Just as we create negativity for ourselves, we can create joy and peace.

Living from the true essence of our self means the end of all suffering and the conscious choice for peace, joy and love, which are the natural qualities of our very essence. This divine, authentic essence is far bigger than the petit, self-created psychological reality of our identity.

Merging with our self means the end of all suffering and fears, including the fear of death. Our body will perish together with our identity but our essence is immortal; it is the same awareness that observes and sees everything clearly, and it will keep evolving within the play of life in different forms and dimensions.

The end of our prejudices, opinions and false beliefs about ourselves and others marks the beginning of our fusion and flow with the self and with life. It marks the end of the limited, disconnected identity and the beginning of a life wherein we are one with every human creature—wherein we are all connected.

It is my wish and my blessing that you can recognize the false beliefs about yourself that keep you trapped in suffering. I hope that that you can realize that you are a beautiful, complete being who doesn't need anything or anybody, much less the acceptance of others, to live in freedom and joy. We are all divine creatures with an unlimited, great potential, which is only waiting to be unfolded in its totality. The place is here. The time is now.

Fifth Myth to extirpate from your mind:

I am not enough.

Substitute it with:

I am a complete, divine and powerful being. I am equipped with everything that is needed to live life in freedom, joy and success. My possibilities are endless and I can sculpt my life the way I want.

HERE is HOW...

Practices & Tools

Find and Question Your Negative Core Beliefs

As we've learned, negative beliefs are mostly subconscious; they go back to impactful experiences in our childhood and most often display a repetitive character. During the course of our life, we find situations to validate those deep-rooted beliefs instead of focusing on what could invalidate them. We repeat this until the beliefs have found so much validation that they become the foundation of our thought process and, consequently, the foundation of our life.

The negative core beliefs are an assumed reality that we believe to be really true. By believing them, we limit our possibilities to act within the true reality of life. If, for example, I hold onto the false belief that I can't move a lightweight flower vase across a table, I will not be able to do it, even though in true reality, I could move it anytime.

The worst part is that when we give credit to a false belief, we create a vibration in the universe which summons evidence to prove it. This is how we perpetuate the same mistakes again and again. It is essential that we take a few hours of our time to discover our negative beliefs and change them. To do this, I again suggest working with Byron Katie's method called "The Work." By questioning your thoughts and going down to the deepest layers of belief, you will find what lies beneath every one of your reactions.

For instance, underneath the negative thought, "I hate speaking in front of people," you may find the belief, "I am not good enough."

Once you have found all the core beliefs which prevent you from being happy and getting the life you want, it is time to question them too, in order to understand they are false. Following Byron Katie's method, you can then find turnarounds or positive beliefs to substitute the negative ones and identify at least three situations that prove the positive belief to be true. For example, if the positive statement is, "I am good enough," you could list, "I can take good care of my life and myself in general"; "I was successful during my school speeches"; and "I am a good teacher." You can then continue to look for evidence that reinforces your new positive belief.

Sometimes we are so addicted to the emotion caused by a negative belief that we are not really willing to let go of the belief. In this case, we really have to be honest with ourselves and understand that the benefits of getting rid of the negative emotion are far bigger than the benefits of holding onto it. For example, if we can't speak in public, we will have many people feeling the same as us and showing us understanding; this could feel safe and attractive. On the other hand, if we are good enough to speak in public, we might create envy or become the target of other people's reactions and judgements—and we might not be willing or ready to bear this situation. It is essential to notice that creating the life we want and being successful is worth this risk.

In the first case, we are dependent on other people's compassion and help and scared to leave our comfort zone. In the second case, we risk going out of our comfort zone, ignore what other's people think and say, and live the magic life we desire. I came to understand that we are judged by people and we become their target, even if we stay in our comfort zone and don't dare doing anything. No matter what we do or don't, there will always be somebody ready to judge or criticize. Remember, most of these people don't have the courage to get out of their comfort zones but would love to be able to.

By questioning your belief, you will find an alternative explanation for what you previously believed to be true. If you believe you are not good enough because that is what your father always told you as child, you might find an alternative explanation for the behavior of your father. Maybe he was unaware and didn't have enough self-esteem and that's why he had to make everybody around him little. His behavior was not personal and was meant to hurt you; this was simply his way to cover his vulnerability. But even if we made mistakes as children, it doesn't mean we are flawed; rather, they were stepping stones to further learning and developing. They don't mean at all that we are not good enough. By replacing our beliefs with a new way of looking at the situation in our childhood, we can very quickly dismantle all of them.

Once we have realized that our negative belief is not true and we have substantial evidence of the contrary, we can use affirmations to anchor the new, positive beliefs in our daily routine until they become the new reality for us. It is quite easy to become the creator of our new reality by simply observing and consciously changing our beliefs and thoughts. By changing our beliefs and thoughts, we also automatically change the power of the connected emotions; the intensity of our emotions will decrease until they finally completely disappear, together with the pain- body.

Chapter VI

ACCEPTANCE: THE SHORTCUT
TO ENLIGHTENMENT

**"If you find all your roads and paths blocked, he will
show you a secret way that no one knows." - Rumi**

I remember when I found out that my daughter was seriously
ill. In that moment, everything in me revolted against this
discovery. Inside of me it turned to winter; a sense of iciness
kept my body stiff like iron and a harsh cold wind inside of me
scattered my thoughts all over the place. A revolt began: "Why
me? Why my daughter? What have I done to deserve this?
What did I do wrong?"

My thoughts became like pointed swords. I turned
unconsciously against myself, torturing myself from within.
It was too painful to bear; I rejected what was happening.
I suppressed my emotions and became like a ghost lost in a
frenetic city. I could not sleep, I could not eat, I compulsively
kept thinking all of these thoughts, which took clarity away
from me. In truth, I needed this clarity to be there, to take the
right decisions, to give help.

There are, however, situations wherein we need to learn
to step back from making decisions and simply keep quiet.

Sometimes the best thing to do is to keep quiet and wait for the solution to unfold.

In my case, keeping quiet was the best thing I could do. I stepped back and let the universe unfold the situation. I realize now that in many cases, this is the only right way to handle something. I had to admit that the universe does a much better job than us when it comes to finding proper solutions for difficult situations.

Fortunately for me, the intensity of the feelings within me became so strong that my body could not bear it any longer, and all of a sudden, I was forced to let go of all my thoughts. As soon as my thoughts slowed down, my emotions became less haunting and the drama took another dimension.

I had reached the point wherein I felt so powerless and so little that I couldn't do anything else but surrender. I had to surrender to the idea of losing my daughter; I had to visualize my life without her, feeling the grief and the sadness swallowing me from inside.

It felt worse than death.

To my astonishment, during this journey within myself, I had to find out that I was strong enough to keep living. I had to learn to let go of everything in life. I had to accept that I could not truly be separated from my daughter because death only affects the body.

Once I saw this, I felt a profound peace pervading all over my person. An endless calmness wrapped me up like a warm blanket and protected me from the cold. I was still and peaceful and I knew that nothing could bring me down again. I gained the certainty that the life within me is powerful, unshakable and endless. I got to touch a space of eternal peace: My authentic core.

This is how I came back to life. Once I did, I found the

clarity I needed to make the right decisions and to be there for my daughter. Instead of fearfully approaching the situation and transmitting this fear to my daughter, I became a strong, unshakable shoulder at her side. Shortly thereafter, after nearly an entire year of struggling, my daughter's health was restored.

This situation, like so many others, taught me not to waste my energy on resisting the situation or the emotions arising from it. Life is a series of happenings and situations, in which we invest too many emotions, thoughts and suffering. These situations are in transition, they come and go again; no matter how mad we get or how much emotional effort we waste, they're going to happen anyway. Instead of wasting our energy on thoughts and emotions, we can use it to face the situation with stability.

Life is a story written for us and it naturally catapults us into evolution. It's going to mold us as long as necessary in order for us to come closer to our truth. Understanding this, the most intelligent thing to do when difficult situations arise is to allow them to be exactly the way they are without giving too much energy to our thoughts and emotions about it, because what we resist will persist. That which we battle with entangles us, while that which we accept frees us.

When we fight a situation, we are in a reactive mode, whereas when we accept it, we let things flow. It's only when things are flowing that we can create our aware response to it. The same is true of our breath: we breathe without having to do or control anything. Just like we need nine months to be born, every change or life situation needs a certain time to arrive and unfold.

Sixth Myth to extirpate from your mind:

We have to lethargically and passively resign to every situation.

Substitute it with:

We simply accept what is. By doing so, we come to a place of peace from which we can take the right decisions and actions for helping others and ourselves. If we become aware and accept what is, we can see things from different perspectives, which enables us to better support others and ourselves in every situation.

HERE IS HOW...

Practices & Tools

Volunteering: The Best Way to Become a Devotee of Life

Volunteering at the Isha Yoga center in Coimbatore was one of the best and most eye-opening experiences of my life. It helped me to understand so many things about myself, others, and how much we are connected—we are the same one energy!

Living in an ashram is not always easy. One time, the ashram got too full and we had to move into provisional shelters in the adjacent fields. I was really bothered by this situation; it didn't meet my expectations and standards. I attempted to resist it, which brought me even more frustration and stress, until I decided to accept what was and try to enjoy it. It was the first time that I clearly and quickly became aware of my resistance, as well as my unease at having to get out of the safe walls of my comfort zone.

As soon as I started practicing acceptance, all of a sudden the walks from the field to the ashram under the Indian sun became a beautiful way to keep myself fit and share funny stories with my friends; the earth that the wind blew into my face became great opportunity to truly enjoy and appreciate the night shower before going to bed; and I came to love the ride back to the field from the ashram at night, on a peasant wooden kind of chariot, squeezed tight between my Indian friends under the beautiful moon. I particularly loved when people walked by, greeting us kindly with joyful smiles. Though the situation didn't change, I changed my thoughts and my emotions followed. This was a true teaching!

I was blessed with the opportunity to teach Judo and Italian to children between six and 13 years old at the ashram school. I am not sure if I learned more from them than they from me. I learned how to drop my perfectionism and my need to be overly prepared, learning to fearlessly enjoy what I was doing; this helped me to be present and truly in touch with the children, inspiring and motivating them. I enjoyed the lessons, having dinner outside while playing and talking to the children, and for the first time, I was having really fun with what I did.

I learned how to be joyful with almost anything, by simply being. Through their eyes always sparkling with joy, and their eagerness to know more and more about everything, the children showed me how authentic and inspired we are when we live from our truth. I learned never to look up or look down to anybody, to drop my judgments, to enjoy what is, and—for the first time—I experienced what it means to be of service: it is pure joy! This kind of happiness is very rare. We feel it by being of service because we act out of our true nature—a core of love, compassion and peace.

There was no space for fears during this experience. I recommend an experience of this kind to everybody who truly intends to transform from an identity into a being. Service is the perfect school for breaking the barriers of our own conditioning and stepping into a deeper dimension of being. But you don't need to go to an ashram in India to have this experience; there are many ways to volunteer. If you learn to devote yourself to service and the life of other beings without suffering the disadvantages that your identity will naturally focus on, you will have rubbed your skin so thin that the space between you and your true self disappears.

Chapter VII

LEARNING TO LOVE

"If I love myself I love you. If I love you I love myself." - Rumi

It was a warm summer, and I was turning over a frozen winter within. I felt like a sleepwalker on a tiny rope, desperately trying not to fall into a bottomless pit, my life unfolding without my permission. Flowers were blossoming, a process not yet allowed to me; I was still learning how to fearlessly leave the seed, a seed I so preciously tried to preserve. My dreams were gone, and so was he.

Living my life compulsively, not really conscious about my false beliefs and my cyclical, negative thought patterns, I was deeply attached to my identity and I really believed that my story was me. I couldn't think of anything else beyond the conditioned accumulation I had become.

Life, which is always very attentive, when it is about to wake up people to their wisdom, inevitably sent me some challenges.

It was time for me to understand that my decisions about life had to come out of a space of love for myself, not out of my fears of the rejection and loss of loved ones.

In my marriage, I was unconsciously trying to extract love

because of my fears. My cup was not full, so I tried to use my family to fill it. By believing that I was not complete, I was looking for completion from the outside and I had already set the trap for an unhappy future.

Most of us behave like this in relationships. When we don't love and accept ourselves, we make ourselves worth less than our partner. This identification with the partner leads us to entanglement and inevitably all kind of fears will follow: fear of losing the person we love; fear of being betrayed; fear of not being loved enough; fear of not being on first place for our partner; but how can we be in the first place when we have already put ourselves second to someone else?

In truth, it is not about first or second, because when we truly love, it is never about measurement.

No one really wants a partner who doesn't have their own life. We don't want others to be dependent on us for their happiness; such a person is sticky and needy all the time.

I became aware that I loved like that; maybe not in that exaggerated way, but I certainly was not an "Individuum", an indivisible unity, and I expected my partner to complete me. From this point, millions of other expectations followed. Let's be honest: most of our relationships fail because we have expectations over expectations. If so many expectations cannot be satisfied by a God, how could they ever be satisfied by a human being?

My divorce forced me to see very clear inside of me and taught me the best lesson in matter of identification and entanglement. Loving without identification is maybe the most difficult thing to do on our earthly journey. This teaching was always very difficult for me to digest because accepting it as truth required me to destroy and let go of my illusionary concept about love and all the expectations connected to it.

Letting go of our conditioned concept about love and life, is the most difficult thing to do for us because we have to give away a piece of our identity, which our ego doesn't like at all. We have to give away this illusion about love wherein a partner does everything for us, cares only for us, dedicates all his time to us, stops going out with his friends, basically stops existing because of us! Personally, I had to let go of the beliefs that if my partner loves me he must not have a reason to talk to other women; he must not be happy without me; he must inform me about everything; and he must kiss me and hug me all the time. With these requirements, the relationship could only fail!

Looking back, I can really laugh about how ridiculous and egoistical my expectations were, as well as about my self-caused drama when I didn't get what I wanted. At the time though, the drama was so real for me that I judged his love based on these tough criteria. No wonder that I needed some time alone to learn to understand, love and accept myself unconditionally before I could truly love someone else. The great irony of this is that when we get to know true love for others and ourselves, we start to want to avoid any sense of bondage; we fall in love with our freedom!

It is important to see that in the name of love, we sometimes become real tyrants. The moment we start to become attached, love becomes addiction and this is not healthy for us or for the people around us. Not only that, but we frustrate the partners who love us and would like to make us happy because they regularly and inevitably fail; our cup has a hole in the bottom and can never be really filled up.

It is beautiful to become aware of the uniqueness of our partners and accept them as they are, instead of unconsciously trying to manipulate them into becoming who they are not.

Don't we want to be loved exactly the way we are? Didn't we wish for that from our parents? So why do we always try to change and manipulate our partners instead of respecting their true being?

It is also true that we never see ourselves as little loving, egoistical tyrants in our relationships; to the contrary, we always think that we are the victims. It is only by questioning our thoughts and beliefs about ourselves, our partners, and love that we can realize that it was about us the whole time: we were busy trying to fulfill our own needs and what we thought was love was actually far from a gift for the other.

I had to be disillusioned and defeated by life a few more times to understand how unconsciously I moved through love and life until I realized the following important lessons:

- I learned to radically love and accept myself, like a mother does with her child, because as long as this didn't happen I was not capable of true love toward others.
- I got rid of all my conditioned beliefs, concepts about right and wrong, judgments, opinions and transcended my entire identity.
- I learned to detach from my story and transformed myself from an identity to a being who lives in the here and now.
- I connected with my true self and gave it my full attention whenever thoughts, emotions and fears desperately tried to take over.
- I consciously realized that I am my authentic self, not my identity.

When I talk about self-love, I don't mean egoistically loving oneself, ignoring others. It doesn't mean we just do whatever we want without caring about anybody and anything else. Instead, it is about developing the necessary love, respect and acceptance for our own self which in turn allows us to recognize the same beauty in others.

If we want to become a gift and a beautiful fragrance for people around us, we have to rub the mud from our eyes first.

Once we can see in the other the same child and adult that we have been and are, we can understand that they are trapped in the same identity and thought-patterns that we are. What follows is that we learn to love from a totally other perspective and with a totally different quality.

It may seem complicated or impossible to reach, but the entire process toward self-love is already a blessing in many ways. We will talk more about self-love and acceptance in Chapter X and see in detail how to kick off the process of self-love so we can keep it going throughout our life.

The way to true love is a process and a path, and if I am walking, everybody else can walk it, too. It is right there; you don't need to go anywhere to find it. Love is *you*. Let's love without fears, with one hundred percent involvement but zero entanglement, as we are complete, divine beings who are perfectly equipped to be happy and joyful on our own, simply from within.

Our partners, children, parents and all the people we are so identified with, are a beautiful complement to—but not the completion of—our self. We don't need any completion as we are whole the way we are. It's our responsibility to create joy, peace and wellbeing within us and make ourselves to the loving, amazing beings we wish to have around us.

Love is not what we do, but who we are.

Once we love our essence, we will automatically love the essence of all the people around us, because this essence is the same in all of us. Let's start now by declaring that you are a powerful and untethered force of life!

Along the way, it's important to remember to:

- Never hate yourself
- Never criticize yourself
- Don't procrastinate
- Don't beat yourself up
- Never be rude to yourself

These are the first steps we can take toward self-love. Be compassionate, patient and understanding with yourself, like a mother to her child. Accept all of you, including the sides that you judge so fiercely. Stop judging yourself for past mistakes because there are no mistakes, only growth steps toward your evolution. We can't do anything more than act out of the level of awareness that we possess at a given time.

Love and accept yourself completely; respect yourself and you will be respected. Never forget that you are the best partner and the best friend to yourself. Fall in love with yourself and others will have no other choice but to fall in love with you!

Seventh Myth to extirpate from your mind:

I need a partner to be happy.

Substitute it with:

I am responsible for my own happiness in life. I love myself and I do the things I love. I am a divine, independent, unshakable self who doesn't need anyone or anything to be complete. I am at ease with my own loving, caring and funny company.

HERE IS HOW…

Practices & Tools

Working with Emotions

The biggest gift of love we can give to ourselves is to learn not to create scary, painful emotions that will negatively affect our life and relationships. But in order to get rid of negative emotions, we first have to learn to get in touch with them.

Most learned during childhood to suppress the emotions we were feeling. We were taught that feeling emotions is bad, weak, childish and foolish, so we suppressed them in order to remain in control of the situation. Over time, we completely lost contact with our emotions to the point that we are not even able to detect them when they arise in our body and mind.

1st. Step – Learn to Feel the Sensations in Your Body

An easy way to detect emotions is to start sensing the physical reactions in our body.

Lie down or sit somewhere alone and feel the sensations in every part of your body, from head to toes. In my case, I sometimes feel jimjams in my stomach, contractions in the upper breast area, a bloated stomach and in general a very tense body. Then I know that I am feeling anxious and fearful about something.

Do this body screening at different times of the day for one week. Write down all the sensations you discover.

2nd. Step – Describe the Emotion of the Sensation

Once you have detected the sensations, try to connect each sensation to an emotion.

For example:

Jimjams in stomach = Anxiety
Contracted breast = Sadness
Tense body = Fear
Bloated stomach = Insecurity, instability, lack of safety

There is not a fixed connection between sensations and emotions; each of us senses a certain emotion in a different way and through a different part of the body.

Do this exercise for one week and write down the results.

3rd. Step – Discover the First Situation in which You Felt a Specific Emotion

Once you have written down the emotions that you feel, it is time to ask yourself: why do I feel this emotion? Try to recollect situations, things or persons that caused you to feel a specific emotion.

For example:

Anxious/fearful = I don't know if it was right to take a certain decision
Sad = I don't understand why I can't find the right partner
Insecure/unsafe = I am so often alone

Now think about experiences from your past wherein you felt the same way. Try to go back to your childhood and find out the very first time you felt that way. By doing this, you will find the root of your emotion, which most of the times is a false belief about yourself that developed during childhood. Now that you are older, you can better understand why you feel the way you feel and where your emotions come from. It is time to understand that they are self-created and to stop identifying with them.

I suggest that you don't dwell too much on your emotions and childhood. There is no need to turn the finger into the wound. It is, however, important to go back and take a quick look at the original situation so you can feel the pain and compassion for yourself. You don't do this in a state of self-pity, but rather in one of understanding, love and compassion for yourself, the situation and the others.

After that, understand that you self-create the same emotions again and again by being triggered by people or external situations. Realize that those emotions don't serve you anymore.

Now, stop identifying with them and try to create more loving and nourishing emotions for yourself.

If you are somebody who doesn't want to feel at all, you are most probably living a lot in your mind and find it difficult to work with emotions at all. In this case I suggest that you try activities that drag you out of your comfort zone and force you to feel emotions. When you experience them, pay attention to them. If you feel uncomfortable seeing a certain person, see that person. If you don't like to watch certain movies, watch them. Pay attention to the sensations and feelings you experience. This can help you to recognize those emotions when they will show up again. Furthermore, they give you the opportunity to meditate on what you don't like, which is where we can find resistance. If we resist somebody or something, we can be sure that we are resisting the emotions they force us to feel. Stepping out of our resistance and trying to understand through the tender eyes of compassion leads us to a happier and fulfilled life.

Create an Exciting Life for Yourself

It is time we start having an interesting and exciting life so we don't feel any need to glue ourselves to others! Above all, we love ourselves, right? So, ask yourself: which kind of life would somebody who truly loves themselves have? Which kind of life do you desire for yourself?

Complete each of these two sentences ten times, keeping in mind that you are the love of your life:

In the life I desire, I am/feel...

In the life I desire, I have/do…

To help you get started, following an excerpt from my lists:

In the life I desire, I am joyful
In the life I desire, I am at ease
In the life I desire, I am of service to people
In the life I desire, I am authentic
In the life I desire, I am loving
In the life I desire, I feel free
In the life I desire, I feel creative
In the life I desire, I feel loved because I love myself
In the life I desire, I feel attractive
In the life I desire, I am spontaneous
In the life I desire, I have nourishing friends
In the life I desire, I have time for myself
etc.

Once you have compiled this list, think about actions with which you can quickly start having those things in your life:

For example:

In the life I desire, I have nourishing friends
Actions: Join a dance group, look for a band to sing in, join a writers circle, invite someone over for dinner

In the life I desire, I have time for myself
Actions: Keep at least two hours free every day for myself, spend time with my art and music every weekend

In the life I desire, I feel creative
Actions: Paint, dance alone, read poetry, listen to vibrational healing music

Don't worry about whether the actions will be feasible or not considering your actual daily routine. Write down everything you can to get nearer the life you desire, and you will see how, consciously or unconsciously, you will start creating time for it.

If you are looking for ideas about activities you could do to nourish your life, check out my website or Facebook page. I regularly organize funny, creative workshops and events through Inner Management, such as workshops on the healing power of sound, art and creativity (painting, writing, reading, design), health and food, yoga (yoga retreats and workshops), and soon you will also find my own yoga clothing collection there! It was my biggest wish to create more places and opportunities for people to be with their self and do art and other creative activities in a conducive, inspiring atmosphere.

I also disliked that it was hard to afford many of these activities. That's why my activities and courses are affordable for everybody. I also encourage you to contact me if you want to join any workshop and activity by just giving a little donation of your choice.

I am open to it, as my purpose is to give everybody the opportunity to experience Inner Management and live a joyful, fulfilled life.

Chapter VIII

ABOUT COMPASSION

"Listen with ears of tolerance! See through the eyes of compassion! Speak with the language of love." - Rumi

When I thought life had beaten me down completely and nothing worse could happen, I had to experience the death of my father. The relationship with my father was always contradictory. There were both hate and love but it was also full of attachment, as almost all daughter-father relationships are.

My father died of an invasive cancer within three months of diagnosis. I was living in another country and my attempts to take a sabbatical time to be able to go and support him came too late; he died before I could leave. Nevertheless, I was able to go and visit him during the three months before he died.

The last time I saw him, he was almost leaving his body. The strong ego was leaving, and what was left was a vulnerable, beautiful being. Seeing him that way, I felt ashamed of having being able to feel angry at him at all.

My father was a man with a huge ego but very soft inside. He couldn't hurt anybody—in reality, he was very vulnerable—but he put on the mask of a rude, strong, undefeated man, which made it hard for people to love him. Totally unconscious, he was one of those men who believed that being strong means not hugging, caressing or giving presence to someone. This was the only way of loving he received from his parents; it was all he knew. He couldn't have done differently, which is why I don't hold bitterness or resentment against him. But during puberty, I was full of rage, anger and resentment because of him. I often had little fights with him and confronted him about his rude behavior.

I couldn't understand how a father could be caring, working and supporting his family while still being so intimidating, stressful, and unkind to those he loved. At that time, I idealistically believed that if I showed him his weaknesses, he might transform his behavior for the best. Now I know that we can only transform ourselves.

I always wanted people to become the best version of themselves, included myself. With the time I understood that everyone, including me, is unique and perfectly divine within. Once I realized how to love myself radically, I understood that there is no need to change or fix myself or others. Now that I have learned to accept and love myself, I am constantly touched by a feeling of compassion about all beings that, like me, are trapped in the unawareness of their own identity.

I now know that there is nothing to change, as we cannot change what is not real. Instead, we can love and be compassionate, accepting ourselves and others for the uniqueness of who we are. Everything and everybody has a role to play in life; nature has planned things perfectly and nothing is there by chance or without a specific role.

Our purpose must be enhancing our awareness, and fixing

situations or people will naturally follow. Life will take care of it. This awareness can lead us from *there is me, and separate from me, there are the others*, to *the others are me*. Once we reach this awareness, there is no longer any need to preach what is right and what is wrong; the right things will happen automatically.

Everybody lives life at a different level of awareness, everybody is on his path; some are at the very beginning of the path, while others are further along. But we all are on the same path with the same skills and uniqueness, as well as our weaknesses and distorted projections about the others.

My father's death made me understand that there is no bad and good or right or wrong in people. All of us are in this journey called life, and we all have the same goal: to reach happiness. Some try to become happy by making lots of money and controlling others, some become happy by helping other people or by becoming spiritual, while others think that if they rob and rape they will become rich, successful and happy. All of us are acting with the purpose of reaching our happiness; we just do it in different ways.

Life is the path for each of us to understand what we truly are, what really matters, what happiness is and why we are on this path. It is a piece of life experiencing itself.

We need to be straight with ourselves and know that even if we think we are good people, we are only good as long as no one disturbs us with something we don't want. As long as others behave like we want, we are good, but if this changes, we can become very nasty and controlling.

If you are somebody who always thinks you are right when you argue with others, I invite you to question your thoughts and beliefs very sincerely. If you have the courage to sincerely look, you will discover that you are not any better than the other and that your ego is contributing to suffering. It is always one's reasoning against another's; only the person who reaches a high level of awareness is able to see both ego games at work for survival.

By seeing, we can consciously choose to behave differently, being the one who contributes to connection instead of reinforcing disconnection.

Once we are aware that good and bad are present in everybody, we can choose to feed ourselves with good. By doing so, we enhance our awareness level.

As a consequence, our awareness leads us to be increasingly realistic and compassionate about other people and their behavior.

We need to drop our concept around morality and look at life neutrally, simply the way it is. And remember: people who think they are good and virtuous are the most difficult and boring to live with! No matter if they're good or bad, both are life!

Through the death of my father I realized that the true self is always unique and radiant beauty; people's behavior is only a projection of their mind, thoughts and emotions. What is important is the thoughts we use to consciously feed the mind; the choice is between nourishing, positive thoughts that serve us or nasty, negative thoughts that lead us to unhappiness and guilt.

Before, I could not understand how my father could be so unaware. Now I feel compassion for a man who was stuck inside the limitations of his mind and identity. These limitations came from his beliefs, education and religion. Now I simply see a man who couldn't see himself and didn't know how to come out of the bondage of his identity. I came to understand that the people who seem the most difficult to love are the ones who most need it.

In fact, I feel compassion not only for my father, but for all the unaware people that I come across in my daily life.

This gives a great depth to my life and enhances the quality of my exchange with other people. It feels good to have the freedom to decide who I want to be and how I want to react; it makes me reside in a space of peace and understanding that enriches my life in a beautiful way, giving it a meaningful depth. It is my wish that you may enhance your perception and awareness to the point that you can be the one who sees things like this.

Once we learn to see things like this, the way we behave with ourselves and with the people around us will completely change. We will discover love for ourselves and for others; we will experience this other kind of love which will turn our everyday life into a much deeper and more meaningful experience.

Let's move the way we want to see the world moving; let's be what we want others to be with us. Let's move from loving only our partner, child, mother to extending our limitless love to every human being that crosses our road in life.

All the challenges in my life were meant for me to rub my skin thinner; to enhance the way of perceiving life and people; to become aware of life and what matters; to become more loving, and less judgmental toward myself and others.

This doesn't mean that we have to be always nice and good; it means that we react to each situation with awareness, the way the situation and the person requires. This is something I really want to stress because lots of people think they always have to be nice to everybody. I also thought so! Your purpose is to react to each situation the way it requires, with awareness instead of compulsivity. There is always a way to show people when they are wrong without having to disconnect. It's hard to achieve, but this is the only intelligent way to go through life. I know it now.

Don't fear being vulnerable. Your strength is in your vulnerability. The key to get through life without suffering is in awareness; enhance your awareness consciously so that it will not be necessary for life to bring you too much suffering to rub your skin thin. Transcend everything you think you are and become who you really are in the core of yourself.

It is from ruins that the most beautiful temples were built; I thank all my challenges today because they made me the person, I am.

May you stay open and receptive to everything that supports and enhances your being and life.

Eighth Myth to extirpate from your mind:

Being compassionate is weak. By being compassionate you get misused.

Substitute it with:

Being compassionate doesn't mean feeling pity for others or oneself; it is more the state of being aware and learning to see with the eyes of the heart rather than those of the mind. Compassion is who we are and is a sign of power and alignment with our true nature. If we love and have compassion for ourselves, we will automatically love others and being capable of feeling compassionate about them. Nobody can misuse us if we don't misuse ourselves. Through awareness and compassion, we reside in our unshakable self. This is stronger than identifying with our shaky identity.

HERE IS HOW...

Practices & Tools

The 5 elements: the basis of our creation

Compassion is something we are capable of being only when we are aware, balanced, free of fears and in joy and harmony within ourselves. A great way to reach this equilibrium is to understand the importance of, and to learn to master, the five elements in our bodies.

The human being as a microcosm and the universe as a macrocosm are both basically made up of five elements: earth, fire, water, air and the space, which keeps them all together. The way we maintain and consume those elements determines how magical and balanced our life will be. It also decides if our body will be a step-stone or a hurdle on our path to wellbeing. Furthermore, by treating the five elements with devotion and respect, we can change the fundamental structure of our bodies and enhance awareness.

Let's have a look at the elements and at what we can do to keep them in balance and working in harmony with each other:

1. Water

72% of our body is just water; this is in sync with the planet, as approximately 72% of the planet is water. The nature of the planet is manifested in our bodies in many ways.

Instead of pouring water unconsciously into our bodies out of plastic bottles and other containers, a simple thing we can do, is to maintain water inside copper containers. Water has a different molecular structure when it has been kept unmoving for a while, which will keep our mind quite rather than in turmoil. Furthermore, copper is a metal with high disinfection capacity and naturally purifies the water from toxins and other kind of impurities.

Treat water with devotion and respect: at least once a day before drinking, thank water for keeping you and the entire planet alive! Put together your right and left palms and bow down to such a fundamental element. You don't need to do it physically all the time; once your awareness is high, you can also do it within yourself.

It is very important to consume mainly fruits and vegetable as they contain high percentage of water. Fruits have a water percentage around 90% and are perfect to cleanse the water in our body; vegetables, which contain around 70% of water, also help us to well maintain the water element in our body.

Spending time around rivers, lakes, seas and ocean or any other water is also a beautiful way to harmonize this element.

2. Earth

12% of our body is earth. The food we eat is nothing else that a product coming from earth, transform itself into the body and life we are. Isn't that a miracle?

It is unnecessary to say that to keep this element in balance the choice of food we ingest is crucial. By eating more water-based food and less dead food, like meat, we automatically enhance the energies in our bodies. To consciously choose a vegetarian diet is to consciously take care of the elements and their harmony in our system.

Another thing that balances the earth element within is being in touch with the earth. Living in cities, we have less contact with earth and mud. Walking barefoot on the ground, planting flowers and trees in the garden, getting a mud-treatment, or trying some grounding techniques are all ways to keep the earth element in harmony. Contact me via the email at the end of this book or on my website if you want to receive free information and description of some effective grounding techniques.

3. Air

6% of our body is air. We can cleanse and maintain well air in the body by simply learning to breathe with awareness. This is why the breathing exercises in yoga are so important. Unfortunately, the air in our cities is increasingly polluted, which takes away the balance. A good thing to do is to search for natural places with lots of vegetation and clean air and spend as much time as possible there. Being in nature is the best way to restore the air element. The trees will gift us with the air exchange we need in a gesture of pure love, in a universal scheme where all is one and everything takes care of everybody and vice versa.

5. Fire

Fire makes up 4% of our body in form of body temperature and life force.

The fire element is automatically regulated by the right managing of the other elements. To keep this element in balance, light a candle every evening before sunset and leave it on for a few hours. You can also stare at the flame for some minutes or bring the flame near your *third eye* (the space between your eyebrows).

Whenever possible, take part in a campfire; this is a great

opportunity to get energized by the fire, the nature and the energy of the other people present.

4. Space

The remaining 6% of our body is space. We don't have to bother about space unless we want to explore mystical dimensions of the existence.

To bring reverence and bow down to the space is enough; at least once a day, in the awareness that space keeps our bodies and all the universe together, put your palms together and thank the space for holding you in perfect balance; this aware gesture alone can open up great possibilities.

The five elements we are made of are very complex and contain memories and patterns from the past, which can easily lead us to compulsiveness and hinder our growth in awareness. The organization of the five elements in our body decides how stable and strong our body is and how tough or easy our path to transformation will be.

I gave you just some ideas for how to master the elements, but there are also rituals and mudras (gestures which can be done with the body, hands and fingers) for the handling of the five elements. For more information about the cleansing and mastering of the five elements, feel free to contact me via the email at the end of this book or on my website.

Chapter IX

FEAR AND ME

"Move, but don't move the way fear makes you move." - Rumi

Like a poison, you crept into my body, filling it with unease. You haunted me in the happiest moments, turning me into an insane being. I swore a thousand times to stop you from weighing on my life, and a thousand times I failed, until I looked from a distance and saw my own radiant light.

I then burned my identity and made space for my graceful self.

I am a creator. *Fear* will never again be the title of my story; instead, it will be *Freedom*.

I spent a good part of my life with the fear of rejection and of losing loved ones. The fear especially haunted me when I was in a relationship with somebody I truly loved. I am not talking about a simple fear, but one that took over my entire body; when it arose, I felt like I was on a torture bed with a vice squeezing me until I could no longer breathe. Whenever I thought I would lose somebody I loved, millions of negative thoughts and beliefs bubbled up like a terrible devil burp, giving life to a myriad of big demons. I became completely imprisoned within the grip of these negative emotions.

I hated my fear so much that when I started losing the people I loved because of it, I thought it was responsible for my misery. I didn't realize that it was not fear that was ruling my life, but that I was the one unconsciously creating this pain and hurt for myself. I, and I only, was being so unloving to myself by scaring myself with an unrealistic, self-created fear that never corresponded with real-life facts.

Over time I also came to understand that the solution was not to curse the fear and make it responsible for my unhappiness, because a negative approach to fear is counterproductive. This is true of every kind of fear or phobia; the same mechanisms and patterns apply, regardless of whether it is fear of rejection, fear of flying, fear of losing loved ones, fear of spiders or fear of death.

The fear only started to disappear in me when I became aware that I was responsible for causing myself to feel it—when I understood where it came from and why. Then I could feel compassion for myself as a child and adult, and I consciously started wishing for my fear to come and show me the ghosts I still believed in. It was only at this point that I could stop resisting the emotions at the root of my fear and become willing to feel them.

The vibration of fear is one of the lowest we can find in the universe and as such, it creates realities on the same vibrational spectrum. It's no wonder that during the course of my life I attracted many situations and men that mirrored back the same vibration to me.

I began to choose men who would not threaten my safety zone. After some years passed and some relationships failed, I met a man who taught me to re-open my heart to love again. The universe was again being generous; through this man, it offered me my perfect mirror.

My fear was still there when I met him, and of course it became stronger and stronger the more I attached to him and to the thought that I didn't want to lose him. What was different this time was that my partner had a good level of awareness and understood my unconscious behavioral patterns and my fear. He responded with great patience, continually offering me situations from which I could learn to trust, and I started to slowly transcend my fear.

Then, one day, a situation awakened me from the dream of my fear and set me completely free from it. You may find it silly that I reacted to this situation in such an exaggerated way, but people who suffer from fear will understand me, because no matter how silly or important the trigger is, the mechanism of fear is always the same.

It was a sunny day, but there was no sun within me.

I had a fight with my partner and after a day of silence, I called him to reconnect. I can still remember the pain and the knot in my stomach when, to my surprise, he didn't answer the phone. He always took his phone with him, so I started getting anxious. An hour passed and he still didn't call me back.

I was sure that he was tired, he was rejecting me and I had lost him for good. He had always been open and available for a new start after previous fights. At this point my mind was triggered; I started to replay a horror movie scenario over and over in my mind, filled with really ugly images. In retrospect, I can see how unkind I was to myself!

I broke out in tears, desperate, like a little baby left alone by both of her parents. I lay down on my sofa like a fetus in her mother's belly with no air to breathe. Then I experienced a sort of enlightenment; I observed my lifeless body on the sofa as if I were outside of it. I saw this poor body and this identity reduced to a big wound and compassion overwhelmed me. I saw how I was hurting myself with the belief that I was not enough and needed a partner to be complete and exist happily. I suddenly understood that this was not true. I felt the power and the beauty of my true self. I observed with compassion and understood my own limited identity without judgment, accepting and knowing that I was not it.

I looked down at my inanimate body from above and I felt that everything was okay and that I didn't need to fear anything. I knew that my true self was unshakable and strong, that the fear was self-created, and that I didn't need my partner to survive and live happily. In fact, I realized that it was the belief that I wouldn't be able to survive without my partner that made me suffer—a belief I had never questioned. I came to understand that it was time to unconditionally love and accept myself and start valuing the fragrance and the beauty of my true self.

I put my pieces back together. I stood up and decided to spend as much time as possible with myself in silence. I sat in silence for long periods of time and the more I got in touch with the beauty, peace and loving essence of my true self, the more I fell in love with it. At the same time, I started living my own life independently from my partner and engaging with the things I loved, especially the grace and beauty of creative activities. I began to integrate everything I loved into my daily routine: writing, walking in nature, painting, teaching, beautiful sunsets, the ocean, and much more. I consciously tried to not meet too many people, only a few nourishing friends, and I tried to not give energy to my thoughts. When thoughts arose and tried to take away my balance, I sat again in meditation, being able again to observe and distance myself from all that noise.

The more I did this, the more I found I could easily create stillness and balance in my mind and reside in my true essence.

I have learned to love silence, because silence is also conversation: A conversation with the purest intelligence within us. I have learned that I don't have to do anything or be any particular identity to be and exist in my perfection.

We need perseverance in learning to contain the mind, but once we have done so, we can drop any effort and simply be in the beauty and peace of our true self.

The strange thing is that, the more I am silent and in touch with myself, the more I desire to engage only with what I truly love and what matters to me—not because I must, but because doing so gives me an immense joy and makes me feel that I am in alignment with what I am.

I am at complete ease now. I live at my own pace and I feel perfect without any need to add anything. In the space of my true self, there is no past and no future but only now, and in the now, everything is perfect.

Thoughts come and go. They bring us up and down, they change, but our being-ness does not. We can let go of our thoughts and hold on to the unchanging self.

This realization, the realization of our authentic self, is the greatest gift and service we can give to ourselves and the world. Once we have realized this truth, we are free from fear and the grip of any other conditioning.

In this process, fear became my best friend, because through it, I was literally forced to face, overcome and transform all the negative, unexpressed emotions that were stuck in my body, preventing the positive energy from flowing and creating the reality I desired. Fear helped me achieve a quantum increase in awareness and step over to the next level of evolution as a being.

Life will keep challenging us until we are completely free

from suffering and stable enough to live without fears. It will push us to enhance our stability and the capability to surrender to what is, no matter which happens. It does this until we have reached enough self-love and trust to live beyond suffering; until we have learned to trust the process of life, knowing that life is friendly and that nothing bad can happen to us beyond the thoughts we believe in and identify with.

So, when we are overcome by suffering and painful emotions, we can try to consciously work through it with the following steps:

Step 1:

When fear, confusion and negative emotions arise at full speed, try to sort out the pain and all emotions connected to it through meditation.

Step 2:

Fearlessly invite all the negative emotions and allow yourself to feel the pain without giving in to it.

Step 3:

Understand what triggers those emotions. I came to see that I did not suffer from most situations themselves; rather, I suffered from the thoughts and beliefs I had about myself and the situation.

Step 4:

If you are caught up by doubt, self-blame and self-hatred, stop giving energy to those self-destructive emotions. Recall your self-love and observe that these emotions are not true; they are merely what your identity believes in. It is very unkind to yourself to cause suffering by believing in such false beliefs and thoughts, so feel the strong essence that you are and step back to more loving thoughts.

Step 5:

If fear arises, don't give it too much energy and it will disappear very quickly. Fear is just the product of what you are causing to yourself through your false beliefs. See that fear is an illusion too.

Step 6:

Do not resist the situation and the emotions. Accept what is and wait for the emotions to move away—and they surely will. Meditate, pray and let the situation unfold. Trust that the universe is friendly and will offer the best solution for everyone involved.

Situations will always challenge us, but the degree of suffering will diminish over time and in direct proportion with the level of awareness we reach. Eventually, negative thoughts and emotions will completely fade away and a life without suffering will appear. This is the end of all fears.

Let's have a look at the repetitive patterns that generate fear so that we can easily disclose them during meditation:

1. Somebody behaves toward us in a certain way or some other situation that scares us occurs (e.g. my partner doesn't have time for me)
2. This triggers old memories that are stored in our body and mind (e.g. my parents didn't have time for me as a child)
3. Memories are connected to thoughts and emotions we have felt in the past in a similar situation (e.g. I am all alone, I am in danger, I am transparent, nobody cares about me or loves me)
4. These thoughts overwhelm us to the point that we can't think about anything else (e.g. I am not good enough, nobody cares for me, I am a failure, I am not worthy of love, I must be wrong)
5. Those thoughts generate the same old emotions, connected to both our memories and our current situation (e.g. fear, sadness, anger, frustration, depression, unhappiness, stress)
6. The thoughts and emotions become so strong that they imprison us in a kind of hypnotic state, during which our intelligence is completely shut down.

Analyzing this pattern, we can become aware of three significant truths:

1. Thoughts and our identification with or belief in them are behind all of our fears. We recycle old memories, thoughts and emotions again and again and again, keep giving them energy, attention and credit.
2. Our fear is our own projection of past or future thoughts. This means that when we fear, we are never in the now—we are either in the past or in the future. Therefore, fear

is not real; it is only a projection of the thoughts and emotions that we believe.

3. Fear is a horror movie that we create for ourselves. We are the ones who can turn it into a comedy!

4. The movie we create is as unreal as the movie we watch in the cinema. What we see is only a reflection on a screen, just as our thoughts are only the reflection of our minds.

I know that being trapped in fear can be very threatening, especially when deep-rooted emotions create real symptoms of physical dis-ease. And yes, I know very well what it's like when our fear rules us to the point that we lose faith and think we will never make it out of it—but this is also just a thought, and we can choose whether or not to believe it.

It is possible to transcend fear! I did it by touching the essence of myself, and you can too. There, in our essence, resides the awareness and stability which leads us to freedom.

Identifying with our identity is the origin of all of our suffering; if we believe we are our story, we will suffer, but if we can break this belief and merge with what we truly are, we are free. We become something far bigger, than our petit identity.

Thoughts change, but you do not. Let go of thoughts and hold on to the unchanging self. You won't find it outside, so turn inward—knock and open the door from within. The self is there, as it always was and it will always be. We simply have to come back home, aware of the magnificence of our authentic nature.

I know that fear depletes your energy and I know that you are tired, but don't give up, because transcending fear is easier than your mind makes you believe. You'll need perseverance to face controlling thoughts, but when you finally merge with your true essence, you can drop all efforts and simply reside in inner joy and peace.

The realization of your self is the best gift and service you can offer to the world, as this is how people can see their true nature mirrored in you.

May this book help you realize that fear is just a thought, not a reality, and that you can set yourself free from what doesn't exist.

Ninth Myth to extirpate from your mind:

Fear is my enemy. I hate fear. I fear it when it shows up. I hate myself for not being able to overcome it.

Substitute it with:

Fear is a self-created, illusory reality which forces us to face the truth about the madness of our mind and pushes the evolution of our being to the next level of awareness.

Don't put up a war against fear; welcome it and its emotions. Realize that fear is only a self-created illusion and it will dissolve as quickly as it appeared. We only need to realize that fear is simply a thought to be believed or disbelieved. Always remember that thoughts and emotions come and go; they are not real, but self-created instead. If we choose not to host them or give them five-star treatment, they won't come back again.

HERE IS HOW...

Practices & Tools

Learn to Abide in the Present Moment

If we see ourselves only as physical beings and reside permanently in our identity, suffering and fear are inevitable. Everything that has a physical form is subject to impermanence and change, as life is constantly evolving; furthermore, form moves within dualities (good/bad, right/wrong, love/hate, sadness/happiness, life/death) and therefore must constantly fight for survival and preservation. This inevitably leads to conflicts, separateness and fears of all kind.

That's why it's essential that we get in touch with the stable, peaceful essence of our true nature, which is not constantly doing or having but is essentially being.

What does this mean?

Fear can exist only when you dwell in the past and the future; the identity is a specialist in never residing in the now. When you are in the moment, in the now, you are automatically in touch with the authentic space within you, which is a peaceful, stable and fearless space. You can always withdraw into this space of lively silence when your identity drags you away from real life, calling you to identify with its horror movies.

There are different ways to practice presence in the moment:

1. Keep your mind free of unnecessary thoughts. Through practicing meditation, you will learn to not give attention and energy to thoughts anymore. All thoughts that don't serve you will be automatically ignored over time.

This state of mind, the freedom from unnecessary thoughts, will automatically raise your energy and free you from all sorts of fears. You'll save the energy now spent on thoughts, emotions and fears and access to higher and higher levels of energy.

2. Switch your attention to your breathing or to any part of your body. This helps turn off the mind. Do it in different moments during the day; simply exercise your power to withdraw attention from the thoughts and into your body/breathing.

3. Be in nature as much as you can. Walk for twenty minutes daily and consciously observe what is around you, whether it be a tree, an animal, a sunset or the snow. Learn to look at these simple things with the innocence of a child. As children, we always resided in our authentic self. Our mind was completely free, which is how we came to see the magic of the things, people, and other creatures around us. Start doing this again. The physical activity will stabilize your body; consciously directing your attention away from your thoughts will increase your awareness and presence in the now, making it nearly impossible for fears to arise.

4. Practice Yoga. You have a physical, a mental and an energy body; fears arise when these three bodies are not aligned. There are special postures in classical Hatha Yoga that, when done very slowly and gently, can help you align your body, mind and energy in a miraculous way. Please send an email to the address at the end of this book for specific advice on those practices or for a trustworthy place to learn these exercises.

Self-Love and Radical Acceptance

When you fear someone or something, you give it energy.

Break the focus. If you are focusing too much on a person, is because you give that person more value than you give yourself.

If you vibrate very low self-esteem, you will attract situations that make you dwell in fear. You need to change the perception you have of yourself, regain power, know what your true self is, and radically love and accept yourself. This way you will be free of fears.

Please refer to the next chapter in this book for more details on how to kick off the self-love process in your life and for practical advice on how to embrace your authenticity and understand the wholeness of your being.

Loving yourself also means treating yourself well in simple ways like:

1. Eating vegetarian food with life force in it. Fresh fruits and vegetable and sprouts are very helpful to increase your energy. The more dead food you eat, the more stressed and fearful you will get. If you eat meat, don't forget that you are ingesting the fear and stress that the animals had to undergo while being killed. If you are suffering from panic attack or extreme fears, I recommend switching immediately to a vegetarian diet. Eating light, hydrating food will make you feel more energetic; you will get in a better shape and feel better about yourself.

2. Don't force yourself into a gym if you love dancing! Do the sport you feel most comfortable with. We don't have to go to the gym if we prefer tennis, kick-boxing, martial arts or swimming. Chose for you what makes you move and is fun at the same time. Your fitness time must not turn into a torture!

3. Stop watching negative news on newspaper and on TV! The news is intended to shock people and create sensation. If

you are anxious or suffer from fears, stop watching the news. You can still quickly update yourself about what is going on in the world by looking at the headlines, but only read the articles that are of real interest to you. Decide consciously where you put your attention and focus; don't let society drag you in the trance of fear. Liberation from conditioning starts from choosing things and people that are nourishing, instead of scaring and paralyzing. Be authentic and choose what serves you and your happiness.

4. Balance your energy body by avoiding energy vampires. Exchange friends and partners who drain your energy by complaining, throwing their bad mood on you, belittling you, using you to feel loved and better about themselves, and expecting too much. Substitute them with people who love your being, nourish you, have common interests and are more aware and stable. You cannot live a joyful life if your energy is constantly depleted.

5. Prepare yourself for bed by making it a time solely for your soul. Ylang ylang oil is the perfect scent for relaxation. It will help release stress and anxiety and introduce you to a good, revitalizing sleep. Put some drops of essential ylang ylang oil in water and switch on a tea candle underneath an hour before going to bed. Then relax, read some poetry or spiritual books, write, or do anything else which creates a graceful space wherein you feel safe and in touch with your true self, avoiding stressful habits like checking email, reading the news or scrolling through Facebook.

6. If you suffer from high levels of anxiety, I suggest you to make use of the audio apps by Glenn Harrold. He offers

hypnosis relaxation and vibrational meditation apps that will help you gradually re-program your mind to a healthier way of thinking, promoting good sleep and inner wellbeing. These apps are not too expensive and really effective.

Face Your Fears Without Judgment

When you become aware that a fear is ruling your life but still you are not able to overcome it, you may start blaming yourself for not being able to cope with it. It is essential that you don't criticize, blame or judge yourself. Be patient and loving with yourself like you would be with your child. There is no need to stress; it will take some time, but you will get out of this pattern. If I did it, you can do it too!

As soon as you start noticing that you are becoming hard on yourself for not being able to overcome your fears after so many years, take back your judgment and feel love and compassion for yourself. Honor yourself for the attempts you are making, trusting that sooner or later they will bear fruit. Remember, even when it seems like you are standing still or regressing, you are still making progress! How do I know? Because I was in this process for so long and I observed consciously every stage and moment of it. I know how it feels and I can tell you that every time you notice yourself feeling fearful, you are actually moving a step further from your fear.

This is why it is so important to meet and feel your fear, including the pain and the emotions connected to it. Each time you do so, you learn something else, and this makes you stronger and more conscious.

So, when you feel fearful, sit in meditation and invite all the bad thoughts, beliefs, emotions and feelings connected to your fear. Allow yourself to feel the pain and the sadness, even if it feels hard. Once you invite the negative, the negative will not have any interest in returning. Negative thoughts only persist when you resist them.

It is essential that you learn to meditate and allow the fear without any judgments or criticism. It is there? Let it in. Accept all the emotions, including the strongest ones, and then let them go. Each time fear and negative emotions come back, they will be a bit weaker, and one day they will stop coming at all. Once you stop judging and fearing them, there is no longer a reason for them to be there. Remember you create them with your attention and energy—so you can also send them away by letting them come, accepting them and letting them pass without giving them new energy and attention.

Also, keep questioning your core beliefs through Byron Katie's method, The Work. It will help you to understand that they are false and become more aware of who you truly are.

I know you are tired, but it's worth it to get to know yourself. Awareness is the way.

Resistance

As we discuss fear, it is of great importance that we spend a few more words on resistance. Whenever we resist a thought and the emotions that come from it, we create fear.

In my constant and desperate search for love and appreciation, I kept changing partners—and since I was stuck in my fear of rejection, of course I kept attracting the wrong ones. I was not really capable of true love at the time, so all of my relationships ended the same way. It was proof of the motto: *If you don't change anything, how can you expect your life to change?* I kept repeating the same two-year cycle.

At the end of one of these cycles, I found myself in emotional turmoil when, once again, had to confess to myself that another relationship was about to end. I suddenly felt an extreme pain in the sacral zone and all along my right leg. The pain was so strong that it created spasms up through my brain. I didn't understand why I was getting this pain; I was desperate, I couldn't walk, I couldn't sit. All of the nerves that passed through the sacral zone were inflamed and I could only bear to lie down on a hard surface. I rushed somehow to the doctor, who promptly told me I had a slipped disk and had to have surgery. Despite the pain, I told him that I wanted to explore alternative methods. He said that we could apply different alternative methods but he couldn't ensure I would heal and, even if I did, it would take a long time.

I felt extremely resistant. I couldn't believe this had happened to me. I didn't know how to handle the situation with my job and I resisted the time it would take to heal.

I went home and started taking pain killers to soothe the inflamed nerves. I had to lie down on the floor of my living room for three long months until I could start physical therapy and other alternative healing methods. During this time, I fought a war against the pain, the illness, the time and myself, causing my nerves to inflame more and my illness not to calm down. As a result, I was causing fear thoughts for myself, envisioning horror scenes about my future that only brought me more fear and resistance.

As the pain became more and more unbearable, I had to surrender, give up my resistance and accept what was. And as soon as I did, I recognized that I could have been doing this all along. I could have been spending this time loving myself, healing and understanding.

I tried to understand why I, an athletic and healthy person with, as one doctor told me, abs one could walk on, had slipped a disk. I then saw that by resisting the emotions connected to ending my relationship, I helped this disk to slip. There is nothing worse than suppressed emotions and thoughts because the body, not knowing how to release and expel them, start moving them into the organs and causes illness.

I was resisting the change in my life and the way my life was. More importantly, I was resisting the illness and all emotions connected to it. Once I gave up and accepted what was—first the change in my life, and then the illness—I started to get better.

The pain began to decrease and I could slowly start to do my physical therapy. Even though every movement ached, I started to enjoy the free time I had for myself. I came to relish the walks to the therapy place because every step was a victory against my illness. I started be grateful for my body and the great way it had carried me up until that point. After a few months, the pain was over and I could walk normally again.

From that moment on, every time something critical happens in my life, the first thing I do is remind myself not to resist my thoughts and emotions but to meet them with compassion and forgiveness. This way I open the door to self-love and acceptance of what is. After that, I try not to give my emotions and thoughts too much energy and attention; thereby avoiding creating harmful fears for myself in addition to my already critical situation.

By giving less energy and attention to our emotions, we stop suppressing them, which is important because this suppression creates more resistance. By accepting and trusting, we create the space for our emotions to dissolve. That's why it is imperative to first observe, understand and embrace them with compassion. Once we understand and accept where they come from, they are automatically healed. Then we can stop giving them too much energy and concentrate on healing ourselves.

It is all about knowing ourselves from within and managing our thoughts and emotions properly.

Chapter X

SELF-LOVE AND RADICAL ACCEPTANCE

"And God said 'Love Your Enemy,' and I obeyed him and loved myself." - Kahlil Gibran

"How could I say something like that?"
"Why don't I think before speaking?"
"I will never get it right!"
"I should not be like this."
"I will never learn."

For most of us, that is what our inner voice sounds like, whether we are conscious of it or not. We are very unkind to ourselves. We nag; we put ourselves down; wish we were different, smarter, stronger, thinner; we wish we were anyone except who we are.

We do this because we have learned to give credit to false core beliefs that we acquired in our childhood and during the course of our life. The conditioning of society and the pressure to always match a certain standard, made us lose contact with our true self and instead develop a schizophrenic mind, which automatically leads us to suffering. We believe these false beliefs to be true and we think they are who we really are; we identify with them, and this identification leads our mind to create negative thoughts and emotions. This is the process of our self-created suffering.

It is essential that we go back to the moment when we began to see those beliefs as real and realize that they were never true.

The amount of love, kindness, depth, support and respect we experience is directly proportional to how much love we feel for ourselves. Moreover, the amount of patience, love and kindness we can offer to others depends solely on how patient, loving and kind we are to ourselves.

Simply put: We cannot give to others something we don't have.

I was always kind of a perfectionist with myself, very critical and judgmental, as this was what I knew from my childhood. I set very high standards for myself, judging others by the same standards—and now I wonder why my daughter is sometimes so critical! By measuring myself against such tough criteria, I was my worst enemy for years, creating pressure on myself, depriving myself the fun, humor and lightness of life, pushing myself to reach a perfection that, even if it were reached, would never be enough. Worse than all of this, I left it to the others to decide if the standard had been met; I left that honor to everybody else outside there, constantly seeking acceptance.

How unkind is that? And what example did I set for my daughter as she grew up?

Being our own harshest critics is very detrimental; we end up judging everyone with the same lack of understanding and compassion, especially if they are different by our standards.

The fact that we now have so many issues of intolerance and so many people condemn simply anyone who is different in creed, race, appearance, etc., has roots in being too judgmental with ourselves.

What about embracing differences? Why can't we embrace everybody on the planet for the unique beings that they are? The answer is that so many of us don't know how to radically love and accept ourselves. No one taught us how. Instead, we were taught that self-love is selfish, that we should never put ourselves first—and this is especially true if you are a woman—that giving is good and taking is bad, that asking for what we need is naughty, that setting boundaries is wrong. Nothing could be more untrue.

The truth is that we can only give love to those around us if we love ourselves unconditionally first.

As a child, I was always encouraged to put myself last, not to be selfish, not to lack manners and never to claim what I needed out loud. I gave and gave away so much that I lost contact with myself and became increasingly unhappy.

Do we have to become sick to understand that this is not the way—that self-love is necessary, and that it is high time for us to nourish our self?

I came to understand that loving and valuing ourselves unconditionally, exactly as we are, is of crucial importance. I saw that we are perfect beings of the universe who are worthy and deserving of love without needing to prove anything, improve or change ourselves in any way. I became aware that we have a birthright to express our uniqueness to its full potential.

I invite everyone who still hasn't consciously kicked off the process of self-love to start right now, and:

- Never let yourself down by not taking time for yourself and the things you love.
- Never treat yourself like a doormat—especially in relationships.
- Never make yourself small so that others can feel big.
- Never put others first, as it teaches them that you come second.
- Never forsake yourself.
- Never forget the powerful self that you are.

This is the greatest gift you can give to yourself and others, because once you truly love yourself, you can be all-inclusive and start loving the entire cosmos.

Live and express your authenticity, because this is your gift to the universe—it's why you came here. Consciously make use of the practices below and you will soon fall in love with the magnificent light of your self. This is why Inner Management is so essential; it helps you tear away all the clouds obscuring the absolute beauty of your true self.

"There is a candle in your heart, ready to be kindled. There is a void in your soul, ready to be filled. You feel it, don't you?"- Rumi

I am again in the authentic space of my self, and I watch a beautiful, strong man date a woman. Both are so different and yet so connected. Magic is all around—the same magic that fills the air when something very special is happening: Two old souls meeting again in this life. It feels sacred; it feels like true love.

A desert beach; a soft breeze like perfumed scent from the universe. Two souls longing for union; two souls longing for freedom. A man at total ease with himself, the ease she longs to reach within herself. He softly kisses her left shoulder while the peacefulness of the ocean embraces them. It is the beginning of an amazing love, a love with plenty of space for self-love, too. And yet, I now know that just as it began, it is bound to finish one day.

The best situation in which we can learn self-love and put it into practice is a relationship. A lot of people believe to know what self-love is, but unfortunately they only know at an intellectual level; when it comes time to consciously apply self-love in real life, we seem to forget what it is and we start selling our soul out. Relationships are the perfect mirror to get to know ourselves in depth and to get our self-love reflected back—if we are willing to see.

The first lesson "self-love" is not to create any expectations. When we expect somebody to:

- Love us
- Respect us
- Be honest to us
- Not lie to us
- Treat us well

We will encounter exactly the opposite. It may sound like a paradox, but it is not. If we need somebody to love us, it's as if we're saying that we need proof that we are lovable.

We don't need to expect love and respect from others if we love and respect ourselves.

The moment we expect somebody to fulfill us, it is as if we gave permission to everybody to make us suffer; we give the power to every unaware person to confirm who we are. In fact, we can only end up being disillusioned, frustrated and full of anger and resentment.

We don't need a partner to prove our self-worth and value and we don't need to prove we are worthy of being respected. Self-love means that we respect ourselves and we know about our self-worth and being love. We must know our value exactly; we don't need anybody to prove it by fulfilling our expectations. As long as we have expectations, we have not yet understood our value.

We need to understand that when somebody is dishonest, they are unaware; they are not loving themselves. Someone else's dishonesty does not indicate that we are not worth honesty. If we stop believing the thought, "I need his/her honesty," we are free. We won't suffer from our partner's lies and cheating and, most of all, we will not attract these lies with the low vibrations of fear—vibrations that want to repeat a situation to prove that our fear and doubts will come true.

It is indispensable that we stop caring about what other people think or believe and how they behave. This is not to be taken personally!

We know we are worthy, valuable, lovable and true. Nobody can touch this; no one else's behavior can ever change this.

If we're being cheated on, somebody is helping us awaken into more self-love and awareness. We are invited to look more sincerely into either our thoughts, emotions, fears or into our unloving behavior toward ourselves. I know you don't like to read that; I didn't either, but as I said before, the truth is not always nice.

It is essential that we start giving ourselves the love, respect and honesty we always wanted from our parents, partners and all those unaware people we met along the way. The time is now.

But what exactly is self-love?

Our first act of self-love is to be straight and sincere about people, life, relationships and ourselves. We can learn to see things and people exactly as they are without changing them into something or someone else to fulfill our needs.

We often know our partner's weaknesses, but we keep seeing what we want because the truth is too difficult. Honesty may require us to decide whether we really want this partner or to re-shape our expectations for the relationship. We have to take over responsibility for our happiness; we have to make a decision, and we don't like that! We prefer to keep dreaming until reality forces us into responsibility.

However, we must see and accept what is; we will not get anywhere if we want to push people and relationships to change so they fit our unrealistic expectations and self-created reality.

Another essential point about self-love, is living our own lives without mixing ourselves into everybody else's world. How many times have we entered the world and decisions of our partners unsolicited?

Loving means leaving the person we love to make their own decisions based on what's good for them, not what's easier and safer for us. Manipulating our way into decisions that don't have anything to do with our own life is simply egoistical. My world and life have to be so beautiful to me that I don't need to enter into my partner's decisions unless I am asked for loving advice. The creation of an amazing lifestyle full of nourishing friends and activities is a *must* for self-love. Once we are in love with the life we live, we don't need to mix ourselves into in the lives of other people.

Another essential responsibility is to not create any stressful and ugly thoughts in our mind. When ugly judgments about a person or partner run at high speed in our head, we need to stop giving them energy; it's essential to slow down and clear up our mind and consciously decide to be and act exactly as we want the other person or partner to be and act with us. Following Byron Katie's method, The Work, let's try to turn around some of those possible thoughts:

- I want him/her to understand me – I understand him/her
- I want him/her to be honest – I am honest to myself and him/her
- I want him/her to care about me – I care about me and about him/her
- I want more harmony – I contribute to more harmony by not creating unnecessary problems
- I don't want him/her to betray – I don't betray myself and him/her

These are signs of an aware and self-loving self. To be self-righteous and want people to behave one hundred percent the way we want is not love. Every time we catch ourselves defending, attacking, or reproaching, we can be sure that we are extracting love instead of giving it.

I know that when it's about betrayal is particularly hard. But if we take a closer look, we can see that people who betray their partner are being truthful to themselves. They are acting by following who they really are. In reality, I am being untruthful to myself whenever I think that someone else has to be different. One partner's betrayal doesn't have anything to do with the other partner's worth; but if we are deficient in self-worth, we need somebody to prove it to us, and we suffer when that doesn't happen. If we know who we are and we have self-worth, who cares if our partner betrays a beautiful partnership? It is that person's problem and has nothing to do with our worth. Our only action is to open our eyes to the truth and decide whether we want to leave or stay; and if we decide to leave, to do it with the least amount of disconnection possible.

Another great lesson in love is to accept that we don't own anybody or anything in this life and that we will have to give everything back to Mother Earth—including our body. Our partners are a gift and an offering from life, and when we receive a gift, why analyze it? Why not enjoy it thankfully?

We have to drop the idea of wanting to own a person, because that person is exactly as free as we are. When it comes time for a change, we have to be ready to accept it and let go. Our partner may want to move on to someone else or live alone; our partner may even die. No matter what the cause, we have to learn to give back the gift we had the chance to enjoy and be with for some time. Likewise, we have been a gift to our partner, giving our presence, grace, joyfulness and help. This is what we are here to do on this earthly journey.

We cannot just keep taking in life, but we can always give. We can give our presence and joy, being someone that makes everyone else's life better.

We only have to remember that we are our own best friends. Just as we trust our best friend's advice, we can learn to trust what we know is good for us and what makes us happy. It only seems difficult because fear obscures our awareness. Once we love ourselves, there is no fear anymore, as we will only choose people and situations which are really nourishing for our happiness. We know how precious we are and will not give ourselves away for anything less.

Essentially, loving ourselves gives us the ability to love somebody else.

If we are in the space of expecting, fearing and needing proof, we are telling the universe that we are not worth enough. In return, the universe will keep sending us the same people and situations until we understand that we are complete, beautiful beings who don't need anybody to give us anything.

We are love, respect, beauty, honesty and harmony. Once we understand this and merge with what we are, we can truly love.

If you are thinking all of the time:

- He/she is an egoist
- He/she doesn't respect me
- I am not worth enough
- I need money, this, that
- I need a man/woman in my life
- I need self-realization
- I need a better job
- I need him/her to say that...

Remember that this is the mind of somebody who hasn't realized yet their own true self and thus believe that they need everything all of the time. Never believe those thoughts, because they are only projections of your mind in its attempt to control reality.

Instead, try to be your true self:

- Love
- Respect
- Self-realization
- Abundance
- Peace
- Beauty

And love what is!

How do you recognize that you are learning to love and accept yourself and your true nature? You may notice that:

- You start loving being alone home doing what you love
- When you think back to your past life, relationships and people, you feel full of compassion and understanding
- You don't have any interest at all in other people's judgments
- You stop extracting and you start giving in relationship to others
- You can love others truly; people around you will smell it and, consciously or unconsciously, feel attracted to you.
- You don't have any unrealistic expectations for yourself and in others, which exponentially increases the quality of your relationships

As human beings, we are very capable of love; we can love our own children, but we can also love a thousand other children. There is no limit to our love unless we create one. We can love someone who is not that perfect, we can love relatives despite their oddities, we can see worth in our partners despite their flaws. We are capable of seeing the beauty in people despite their imperfections. So why do we make it so difficult to love ourselves?

What are you waiting for? Start right here, right now.

Tenth Myth to extirpate from your mind:

I offer myself totally to the other and I expect the other to recognize my value.

Substitute it with:

I offer myself knowing that I am valuable, worthy and lovable and don't need to expect anything from anybody to prove it. I love and radically accept myself, and all of my decisions come from self-love and authenticity. As a consequence, I will attract only loving and authentic beings around me.

I love all-inclusively, without fears or expectations, knowing that I don't own anybody and that all form will at some point change, transform or end.

HERE IS HOW...

Practices & Tools

Creating Self-Love

Since we cannot give what we do not have, loving ourselves is absolutely necessary before we can truly love anyone else.

Ask Yourself:

- How can I love myself more?
- What would I be doing right now if I did love myself?
- What would somebody who truly loves themselves do?
- How can I support myself more through the challenge I am facing?
- How can I be a model for my children?

STOP...

- Saying yes when you mean no
- Feeling guilty when you say no
- Giving up your values and integrity in order to please others or fit to a group
- Keeping quiet when you have something to say
- Taking over other people's ideas and beliefs to feel accepted
- Not calling out somebody who mistreats you
- Accepting sex when you don't want it
- Letting yourself be interrupted or distracted to meet somebody's else need

- Giving too much just to feel useful
- Becoming overly involved in someone else's problems or difficulties
- Allowing people to say something to you that makes you feel uncomfortable
- Being afraid to communicate your emotions in relationships
- Violating your boundaries
- Betraying yourself
- Comparing yourself to others
- Wanting to be perfect
- Resisting what is

Possible Ways to Show Love Toward Yourself

- Make your happiness the first priority in your life
- Always tell the truth to yourself
- Honor your feelings and emotions by observing them from a distance and without judgment
- Recognizing feelings and emotions as important signals that indicate deep-rooted, false beliefs
- Honor who you really are, as you are the only one who knows what is good for you
- Recognize that universe is made of love and if you open yourself to receive, everything is possible
- Surround yourself with the right people and in the right environment
- Be thankful
- Recognize that your fears are nothing else than thoughts you strongly believe in
- Do things you love and which make you feel good
- Laugh as much as you can

- Eat the right food for you
- Create a list of your positive personality traits
- Forgive yourself or, better, understand that there is nothing to forgive
- Realize that it is okay not to be okay; realize that "I am not ok" is just a thought you create and believe in
- Flow with life without trying to control, trusting that you will land on what is best for you
- Ask for help when you need it
- Meditate, write and be creative
- Commit yourself to do something which makes you happy every day
- Be authentic, no matter what people say or think
- Become your greatest fan

You Know That You Are Being Loving Toward Yourself When . . .

- You allow yourself to make choices that feel like fun and that bring you joy and pleasure
- Things in your life run effortlessly
- You are not constantly worrying about what others think or will say about you
- You are willing to easily open to others and are no longer paralyzed when it comes time to act
- You stop feeling guilty when your life is going well and you are happy
- The voice of your self-critic is no longer the loudest voice in your head and you start be kinder and more patient with yourself
- You can accept compliments and respond with genuine gratitude

- You don't fall so easily into entangled relationships
- If you do something for others, you don't do it out of a sense of obligation but out of love
- Your love is no longer restricted to romance but is expanded to everybody else, too

Chapter XI

WHAT IF OUR LIFE PURPOSE IS CONNECTION?

**"Out beyond ideas of wrongdoing and rightdoing
there is a field. I'll meet you there." - Rumi**

I remember the day that my daughter had to be brought immediately to the hospital. I can see the doctor's concerned face before me, his eyebrows falling together as if in deep thought. A cold shiver ran through my body; like a repeating smash on my face, the sound of his words echoed in my mind. I thought of thousand questions but my mouth was not able to speak them aloud.

At this point fear had already overcome me, like poison slowly spreading into the body, suffocating the throat and converting the stomach into a node, hard like stone.

Like a lifeless robot executing an order, unable to hold back my tears, I went out of the room as my daughter's sweet, pale face stared at me. There is nothing worse than having to show serenity when you are dying inside, but a mother always knows how to do things that seem impossible to an external observer.

I knew I had to organize everything quickly while my mind was paralyzed by the thought, "Why her?"

And so, after my divorce, when I had hardly finished

recollecting my broken pieces, when I was still managing a full-time job, financial matters, and trying to be both father and mother for my daughter, life hit me with the next stroke: My daughter became seriously sick. I am not going into the details of those moments which were surely the most painful of my life. Watching my own daughter suffer without knowing whether she would survive was so painful that no words can describe it. I felt incredibly helpless as life taught me what trust is.

I always thought of myself as tough and strong, but life suddenly uncovered all the vulnerability that I was not capable of accepting and expressing up until that moment. It was inexplicable to me why my daughter got so sick, but after questioning and struggling, I came to the conclusion that it simply had to happen. At that time, I didn't understand why, but thinking about it now, I know; I needed to become aware of another huge truth in life: We are all connected.

Throughout my daughter's illness, I came to understand the importance of always staying connected to other human beings and life, no matter what situation arises. We are all one, and if we disconnect from ourselves, we disconnect from others; in the same way, if we disconnect from others we are disconnecting from our authentic self.

After my divorce, my ex-husband and I disconnected completely from each other. I think this is what 90% of the men and women after a divorce do. We go from being loving mothers, fathers, wives and husband, to a bundle of fears and emotions, completely reactive and disconnected from who we really are: graceful beings of peace, love and compassion.

Mind came in, and we hated, we fought, we resented,

we disconnected. As a result, very low energetic vibrations emanated, which surely didn't attract anything positive to our lives. I think that my daughter's illness had a lot to do with those low energetic fields. When such negative energies are released, our children feel it, even if it's never expressed in words or fights. Everybody else around us feels this negative energy too, and the vibrations make us unavailable to enact beautiful changes in our lives.

Moreover, the hatred and negative thoughts we have go out to other people and all over the universe, as the universe is one, and everything and everybody within it is connected. I like to look at the universe like a huge, big hand, where each single finger is unique yet connected.

Through the conflict with my ex-husband, I clearly experienced that we are all one energy.

I am convinced that negative energies and vibrations emanating from the minds of human beings are the cause for illnesses and many conflicts existing on the planet.

Similarly, recent science has pointed to one space of non-physical form that connects everything and everybody with each other—a space where everything was created, which envelops and keeps everything together, and which being no-form cannot be measured by our instruments. All scientific theories around the so-called "God particle" move around the concept of a no-form which keeps everything in place.

In this universe we are more connected than we like to think. Human beings between each other, human beings with nature and vice versa; everything is connected to everything and everybody. Whether we want it or not, whether we like it or not, this is the pattern of life; we are one energy!

The sooner we understand that our vibrations and thoughts are the greatest contribution we can make to ourselves and others, the quicker we will attract the loving and peaceful life we desire. More than that, our thoughts and their energetic vibrations can be a great contribution to this planet and all human beings, as our positive energy has the power to raise the vibrational level of the whole planet, rebalancing the negative fields.

Using kinesiology muscle testing levels, the following human emotional vibration frequency analysis illustrates the vibrational analysis range from higher to lower emotions:

700+ Enlightenment
600 Peace
540 Joy
500 Love
400 Reason
350 Acceptance
310 Willingness
250 Neutrality
200 Courage
175 Pride
150 Anger
125 Desire
100 Fear
75 Grief
50 Apathy
30 Guilt
20 Shame

Every person on this planet is vibrating at a very subtle hertz frequency. When we are joyful and expanding, we move between 200 - Courage to 700+ - Enlightenment. When we are experiencing fear, anger and shame, we are contracting and we move between 20 - Shame to 175 - Pride.

Breaking negative cycles means raising our emotional state by mainly experiencing higher frequency vibration emotions such as joy, love, and acceptance. By consciously choosing to break our cyclical mental patterns, we can create positive emotions for ourselves, which in turn help raise the vibrations of others. The goal is to live life from a place of love as much as possible. When we face difficult situations, it can be of help to ask ourselves: What would love choose?

Living by nourishing the positive within you is a much deeper way of living—a way that helps us reach the purpose we are seeking.

Everybody is looking for a big purpose in life, mostly being of help or service, but one significant thing I came to understand is that the first and most important purpose any of us should have in life is to become joyful and loving human beings with a balanced, clean mind and an inclusive heart. Only beings like this will be able to always stay connected to other people and life, no matter what comes.

We don't necessarily need a big purpose in life; being a connected, loving, caring, compassionate and positive human being on this planet is the most amazing gift we can give the world and ourselves.

Let us consciously sculpt ourselves into joyful beings from within by refusing to let thoughts and emotions drag us away from our true self. Let us engineer our inner world of thoughts and emotions so that we can manage to sculpt a life without unnecessary suffering. Let us get rid of all our likes and dislikes, judgments, opinions, concepts, and identity that we built up around our self. We don't have to destroy our identity; it's enough to learn to step out of it whenever it doesn't serve our happiness.

If I would have been able to step out of my identity and its personal emotional drama and simply embrace my situation the way it was, I could have avoided a lot of unconscious nastiness and suffering for myself and others.

We cannot manage many external situations in life, but we can certainly manage our internal way of being, and this is what we have the responsibility to do if we want to exist as joyful human beings. This is what living our yoga truly means: to be in union with everything and everybody around us at any time and in any given situation.

Make it your life purpose to sculpt from your identity a joyful, loving and compassionate being who is capable of staying connected in any situation.

Eleventh Myth to extirpate from your mind:

To always stay connected, I need to always be good, and this doesn't work in normal life. Furthermore, if somebody doesn't love me anymore, I have to hate them and extirpate them completely from my life.

Substitute it with:

I stay connected, but this doesn't mean that I have always to be a nice person; I can briskly say what I think if the situation or person requires it, and I can decide to leave somebody who doesn't nourish my being any longer without disconnecting at the human level. It means that I don't need to inflict rejection, hate, anger or other destructive treatments. At any time, we can express ourselves peacefully without using words as weapons that hurt the core of the other being. We can also peacefully go away from another being in awareness and in the name of freedom for both; there is no need to treat anyone poorly, judge them or hurt their core, especially because by hurting them, you are hurting yourself. Remember: we are all one energy, whether we like it or not.

HERE IS HOW...

Practices & Tools

Mastering Breath with Awareness

We are only able to connect with everything and everybody if we learn to be intense and 100% involved with the life around us. We fear this because we have learned to habitually distance ourselves from everything, which makes us feel bad instead of observing and transcending this habit.

Fears are responsible for keeping us away from our natural capacity to love and connect with people and life. Living trapped in our conscious or totally unconscious fears changes our inner chemical balance, putting us in a defensive mode. The first thing that changes is the rhythm of our breath, and this starts a negative chemical reaction throughout the body.

That's why it is essential to learn how consciously slow down our breath.

Here is a little practice you can do daily to slow down your breath. It is intended to help those who are just starting to learn breathing techniques.

Sit comfortably with your spine erect. Remain totally still and allow your attention to become still as well. Do this for five to seven minutes every day and you will notice that your breath will slow down.

It seems easy but it is not; your mind will try hard to get your attention. Only when you have mastered the noise of your mind and the shakiness of your body will the breathing start to slow down.

Over time you will see that you can keep your breath even when you are very busy, stressed or angry. You don't need to learn breathing acrobatics; it is enough to consciously train your breath to slow down at demand.

Why is it so important to slow down human breathing?

A human being breathes twelve to fifteen times per minute. If we can keep this on the slower end of that spectrum—perhaps down to twelve breaths per minute—we will enhance our perception and sensitiveness considerably. If we further reduce our breathing to nine breaths per minute, we can understand the language of other creatures on the planet. If we can get it down to three breaths per minute, we will know the language of the source of creation!

Beyond this, our own longevity is related to the rhythm of our breath; the slower the rhythm, the longer the life on earth. That's why turtles, which only breathe three or four breaths per minute, can survive for hundreds of years!

Beyond all of this, slowing down our breath helps us to achieve a certain ease in our system so we can evolve to a state of stability and remain there, regardless of the situations life throws us into.

Mudras

We can also only stay connected to everybody around us if we are capable of transforming our compulsiveness into awareness and balance. A good practice to reach stability in our body and mind is to use *mudras*. The word *mudra* comes from the Sanskrit language and literally means "a seal." It represents a certain hand position which can alter the way our system functions. The most known is the *OM Mudra*, which is the way we keep our hands and fingers during a meditation in the lotus posture and involves touching the thumb and forefinger together. Mudras are a subtle science of arranging the energies in our body in a certain way. After all, our bodies are receptacles for the divine.

To start, try this little breathing exercise. Sit quietly with your palms facing downwards on your knees, staying aware of your breathing. Then, after a few minutes, turn your palms upwards, still with your awareness on your breath. Do you notice the difference?

When the palms are downwards, the lowest area of our lung is activated, and this stimulates diaphragmatic breathing. When the palms are upwards, the middle part of the lung is activated. This part of the lung opens the chest area and the breathing is more open. The life energy in our system can be altered by just changing the positions of our palms!

When we hold a certain mudra, the energies tend to move in a particular way. By holding a mudra and breathing in a specific way, we can send energy to any organ or cell in the body. Hands are the "fine-tuning" instruments for our entire physical construct. Let's look at why.

Mudras and the Five Elements

Each finger of our hand corresponds to one of the five elements in our body:

- Mudras for the *earth* **element will include your ring finger**
- Mudras for the *air* **element will incorporate your index finger**
- Mudras for the *fire* **element will include your thumb**

- Mudras for the *water* **elem**ent will incorporate your little finger
- Mudras for the *ether* **element will focus on your middle finger**

We have already learned about the importance of the five elements in our body. When these five elements are out of balance we get various physical and psychological ailments, behave re-actively and compulsively, and dwell in a state of dis-ease.

Here are some types of Mudras and their benefits:

Mudra for Energy Balance

This mudra, which helps align the elements, is a good place to start. It incorporates each of the five elements by including each finger in the process.

If you are feeling stressed and you don't have much time at disposal, this mudra will help you. This set of four mudras can be done from anywhere and after a few minutes it will rebalance the energy in your entire system.

First, touch the tips of your thumb and index finger together on both hands simultaneously and hold for approximately five seconds. Then, move your thumb to your middle finger and hold that connection. Continue to your ring finger and lastly your little finger. Do several rounds of this until your breathing has slowed down and you are ready to get back to your activities.

Mudras for Emotional Balance

These mudras are meant to help you adjust overwhelming emotions. Each finger corresponds not only to an element, as discussed above, but also to emotions and internal aspects of your body. In order to affect either the emotion or body part, squeeze the corresponding finger on both sides.

- For emotions relating to fear or issues related to the kidneys, activate your little finger.
- For emotions relating to anger or issues connected to the liver, gall bladder, or central nervous system, activate your ring finger.
- For dealing with the emotion of impatience or the heart, small intestine, circulatory and respiratory systems, activate your middle finger.
- For emotions relating to depression, sadness, and grief or issues with the lungs, activate your index finger.
- For dealing with the emotion of worry or anxiety or for reoccurring stomach issues, activate your thumb.

Recommendations

Being an integral part of yoga, mudras must be accurately transmitted; if used to enhance perception and awareness, they must be done in connection with special breathing exercises, etc. Please refer to my website or send me an email to book a specific workshop or acquire specific information on the science of mudras.

Chapter XII

WHAT I HAVE COME TO UNDERSTAND

"There is a voice that doesn't use words. Listen." Rumi

Identity: "What is that you want?"

Self: "I am perfectly content; I don't need anything. I am free from your limitations and all the limitations of the form. I fly high, smelling the fragrance of freedom. I am that.

I am the world in its most sparkling and authentic colors; I am beauty all around, all over. I am a melody coming from the heart; I am a dancer, swinging through the immense space of nothingness! Why do you cry?"

Identity: "Because I am in prison, I'm stuck inside and can't really fly. I also cry because of your immense beauty; it's too much to bear."

Self: "You cry looking at yourself? Why?"

Identity: "You are so beautiful that I can't contain you!"

Self: "You can! You are doing it right now. We are not separated. Why do you create an illusory prison? There is no prison apart from your perception; your perception is your self-created prison. There is no prison until you create one through your thoughts. So stop! We can fly everywhere we want, nobody can do us any harm. We are too colorful for somebody to diminish our spark; the deep violet, the blue and this white glow are so intense! It feels so good to get lost in one's own beauty!

I am everywhere you go, in every person you meet, I am you, I am everything but no-thing. I AM."

Identity: "Don't go away. I want to always stay with you."

Self: "I don't go anywhere. I am you, I am here and you can merge whenever you want; every time you are here and now, I am there. You can inhabit me every second of your life. I am here, simply tune into me."

Identity: "You were always here? I was always there? I felt disconnected only because I lost contact with my beauty. Yes, I see it now. It is so simple. I am going to fly high now, because there is no fall, I am flying high, and my form will follow!"

It is essential to put this right:

We are not a body that contains a self.

We are a self, a limitless essence with a body residing within it during the short earthly journey called life.

The self and the identity are a bit like the wave and the ocean. We think we are the wave, or identity, which is created and dies on the surface of the shore, but in reality, we are the entire ocean, the self, from where the wave comes into being.

The ocean is infinite, the wave is time-bound; the rolling on the surface is what we call life.

The self is capable of observing that the identity, through the mind, keeps causing emotional storms and sorrows. It decides not to get absorbed into this status of no peace; it doesn't identify with it. It can see the nasty mind game. It can see the body and the mind trembling in fear, and yet it remains unshakable in the awareness that it is untouchable, powerful and immortal. We are this awareness; we are the same unchangeable one who observed our identity when we were two, seventeen and thirty years old, and we are still the same one that observes our evolution when we are forty, fifty and older.

When we are unaware, we believe we are the identity and its drama. This is an illusion. When we become aware that the identity is a false self that is made up of mind, thoughts and emotions, a certain delusion takes place—a delusion from the illusion of being who we are not: our identity!

The illusion of the identity continues its course, but once we are in touch with our self, we are no longer identified with it; once we reach this level of awareness, we can play with the identity in the world of illusion while residing in awareness.

Stay in the self does not require effort because the no-form of the self is what we are. This spaciousness of peace and love is our true essence. We can inhabit this space any time we want, without making any effort or going anywhere; we just need to tune in and merge with what we are and what we have always been: the self. There is no distance between us and our self; we are it. We simply got lost in the fog of our mind and in the identification with our identity.

We usually touch the self when we abide in the moment. That's why it is so essential to manage our mind, so that we don't reside always in the past or future; if we succeed in keeping the mind empty and in the moment, we automatically merge with the core of ourselves, with our self.

Silence is the easiest way to merge with our self. Many people think that silence is boring and of no use, but in truth, the best ideas and choices come from the silence and stillness of our authentic self. At the same time, maintaining stillness and equanimity as we perform our worldly actions is what leads to real success in life. That's why we are very lucky if we are able to discover activity in silence and silence in activity. Experiencing this merging of silence and action is the meaning of enlightenment.

Each time we are simply in the here and now, we are in contact with the peaceful, silent, awesome vastness of our self. This space is not a dead, inanimate vacuum; on the contrary, it is a lively space that emanates calmness and peace and from which the best creative ideas and decisions for our life can flow. It is the pure intelligence, from which true life is sculpted. It is the only space that knows what we really love and long for.

To inhabit our self, our divine, immortal essence, means to be in touch with our universal intelligence, uncontaminated by memories and thoughts. When we give too much attention to the identity, we separate ourselves from our own magnificence. It is like having golden treasure in the house but ignoring it.

To dwell in the self means the end of all fears, with the awareness that no matter what happens to the identity, the self will survive as universal intelligence and immortal spirit.

It is in silence that the self can be perceived. Once detected and touched, it will remain with us—even in the most chaotic moments of our lives. In fact, when we act out of the spaciousness of our authentic self, we can consciously take part in the game of identity without suffering our own mind and emotions and becoming stressed by them.

Regardless of how much turbulence the identity invents, the self will remain the intact, aware observer of what is. It will not try to function, solve, or do; it will simply remain in its pure being-ness.

Enlightened beings and sages have reached this unshakable state—a state that each of us can touch. It is possible to attain. It's even easy. We struggle so much to attain to it from the outside in, to feel it through our sense perception. Being that the self has no form, we can never perceive it at the level of the senses. If we open the door to silence, perception and intuition, we can easily merge with the self and understand that it was always there; we are it, we only think that we are separate in the illusory intellectual belief that we need to discover something outside of us. The mind believes it has to apply difficult intellectual methods to discover the truth and that's why it holds on for so long; the stronger the intellect, the greater the self-created distance.

It is almost impossible to explain the self through the intellect and the mind, as we cannot use words and definitions to describe something that has no form. But if we use the antenna of our intuition and refined perception, we can easily tap into it.

Our self is indivisible, complete one. Once we realize the oneness of our nature and we reside in the heavenly magnificence of our self, everything around us is no more than a dream. It loses importance and, consequently, its grip on us.

We are already perfect, but we don't know it yet. To realize our own beauty is a process, not a big bang effect; it is the sum of many "aha" moments through which enlightenment comes. Then, one day, we find that we can say heaven is a state of mind.

When we meditate and observe our mind at work, we think and speak of it as if we are the mind. The observer is at first completely identified with the object it observes.

"I am so confused; I can't stop myself from thinking; I am so helpless." This are all typical statements of somebody who is completely identified with the mind.

How can this happen? How can it be that the observer is not the powerful self, but the identity instead?

We have been thinking and believing for so long that we are

our mind and identity that this belief has completely overridden the self. The self, in turn, waits patiently while we get back to it through the realization of the illusion of the mind-game.

We lost track of who we really are because of conditioning. This is the trance that needs to be broken; this is the dream from which all human beings need to awaken. We need to realize that we are neither the mind, which is made of thoughts and emotions, nor the identity, which is made of opinions, beliefs, judgments and philosophies, but that we are the universal awareness that observes itself playing the game of dualities. When we do this, we can evolve and expand endlessly.

If we observe deeper during meditation, we can notice that we are not this observer, but that the observer itself is observed by another entity. This entity is our true self, which is most of the time amused by the drama of the identity. This entity is what the Hindu culture calls *Shiva*, the immortal, endless, formless, unshakable space, the formless nothingness within which both the play of the identity and authentic life take place.

This space is both where we come from and where we will end up after death. We are this essence that observes both the observer and the object of observation.

When we die, this essence leaves the body through the last exhalation but keeps living in the universe in different forms and dimensions. This is the pure divine intelligence that if touched by a human being, can transform him into a creator—someone who gets what they want without any effort. Every desire will become a reality once we are totally in touch with this kind of intelligence, and even if we are able to merge only with a small percentage of it, it will create magic in our life. This is what most people are trying to reach through spiritual practice.

We are the drop in the ocean (identity) but also the ocean in a drop (self).

We are this huge, divine essence, so why persist in identifying ourselves with the petit psychological reality of our mind and identity? We are a limitless gold mine but we don't know it yet; we think we are limited. And the problem with that is that what we think, we manifest.

To escape human suffering, we have to stop identifying with the form, as the form always changes. Because it is transitory, our identification with it will inevitably lead to suffering. As a form we have to fight, control, do and function, trying to preserve what is transitory in its nature.

Our true self, to the contrary, flows with what is. It simply *is*. This is why the quickest way to touch our essence is to stop doing and talking; by meditating in silence, you can observe the observer and the object and come to experience your true self. This way, realization is not only intellectual knowledge; it's a true experience.

There is no door between our true self and us; there is only the illusory barrier we create with our own minds.

Don't be deceived though; if the body and the mind are the biggest hurdle in our search for the self, they are also the only doorway through which we can get there. That's why it is imperative to understand that our identity is not a part of us to be hated or fought against, but rather an entity limited to the senses. As such, it is not bad, but simply limited.

We need to understand the illusory nature of the identity and learn to disempower, contain and lead it where our true self wants to go—not the other way around. Knowing that the identity is limited and illusory, we can use it, play with it, put on different forms and identities to get through life without getting lost or imprisoned. The way out of your identity is the way out of suffering.

May you tap into the spaciousness of who you really are!

Twelfth Myth to extirpate from our mind:

We are our body and mind/identity.

Substitute it with:

We are the self. Body, mind and identity are external accumulations which belong to us but are not us.

We can merge with the self by enhancing our perception and intuition, being in silence and simply residing in the here and now. Once we touch this pure intelligence within us, we can become the creators of whatever we wish and believe in this life.

HERE IS HOW...

Practices & Tools

The Hidden Sound of Existence

When addressing our reconnection with our self, which is not made of physical matter, it is important to switch beyond the five sense organs and just merge with the silence within. This silence is the hidden sound of existence.

Every form has a hidden sound within itself. Striking a chord will emanate a different reverberation than hitting a drum.

Reconnecting with the self means learning to behold the sound instead of the music. The music is the superficial product of the sound, transformed into form. The sound is the basis, the key from which the music comes.

What does it mean in reference to life?

It means that once we have found the sound of a certain form, we get access to this form. Once we have found the key to access our form, we can also access the form of everybody and everything else we get in touch with. Once we can listen to our reverberation, which is the lively silence within, we have found the reverberation of life, which is the form emerging from this silence.

If we want to access life, we must listen to the reverberation of life and not to the superficial happenings in it. By meditating, we get access to this vivid silence within, a void, which contains the reverberation of life. Tune into it because this is the sacred key to access our and any other form of life.

Learning to cultivate silence will help us tap into our true essence—the essence of our authentic self.

Try to cultivate silence by:

1. Sitting still with yourself
2. Integrating silent moments in your daily routine
3. Withdrawing from too many superficial life activities
4. Not talking too much
5. Being in the moment
6. Walking alone in nature
7. Enhancing perception and awareness
8. Learning to listen to the reverberation of life

Once we have learned to reconnect and merge with our self and are stable enough to reside within it, we will be able to throw ourselves effortlessly and one hundred percent into life activities of any kind.

At this point, mastering our life and situations will be an effortless game, as the pure intelligence of our being is turned on and based on an everlasting and unshakable resource.

In this book, I gave you all the tools you need to access your authentic self. Through willingness and perseverance, you can gain sacred access to the life you desire. The time is now.

CONCLUSION

LIVING FROM THE SPACE OF THE SELF

"Why am I seeking? I am the same as he. His essence speaks through me. I have been looking for myself." - Rumi

This is the story of my identity, the one who believed she was not perfect enough to deserve love and respect, the one who walked through life accumulating material wealth and emotional relationships, the one who adapted herself to everybody and everything for the fear of being rejected.

I am not my identity, though; I am the self, the witness to my story and the blank canvas on which the story could take place. I am the one that has observed the suffering, joy, desperation, illness, sorrows and sadness that the identity underwent in its search for awareness and transformation. I am the one that has chosen this identity to undergo the process of transformation toward liberation—liberation from the identification with the illusory reality of the identity.

I am the one that *is*. I am not my story but the witness to it, and the story is neither good, nor bad, but simply a story.

I am not a split being, part self and part identity. Rather, I am the self and I contain a physical identity that I use to express my truth.

I am gravity and grace. The identity is gravity: Form, physicality, survival. The self is grace: Self, spirit, all-containing spaciousness. It is in this apparent duality that we human beings have to learn to live—an earthly journey that aims to realize and dissolve such duality so we can become one with everything.

This duality is not negative or a contradiction, but rather a game through which we get to understand and accept that all comes from one and expresses itself through one: the self, the same essence in all of us. This is the vast spaciousness from where we come, within which we exist, which we long for, and that we will get to after the death of the body.

The one who is capable of transcending the identity during this earthly journey will know the self and become all-inclusive and one with everything. Transcending the identity doesn't mean ignoring it or rejecting it as negative because of its limited nature, but rather eliminating the strong identification we have with it.

If we reach the right distance from the identity, we can use it for our survival within society without attaching. Once the identification with the identity is no longer there, the suffering will disappear.

It is not about criticizing the identity, denying it and going to live alone in a cave in the Himalayas. This has always been a big misunderstanding; we cannot completely drop our identity, we can only become aware of it, drop our identification with it, and stop giving it too much attention and power. The more we are identified with the identity, the more distant we are from our true self and from existence, dwelling only in appearances and suffering.

The attention and the power must be kept in the self, which has to have the right distance to observe and consciously act.

Our identity, which we have used to fight, control and survive, suffers from this duality a lot. It's afraid to admit the existence of the self. This is because as soon as the identity admits that it can exist only through the self, it admits its own limitation, as there is nothing more to fight about or control once we live in the loving, peaceful and compassionate space of the self.

When we are completely identified with our identity, we develop a sort of existential fear of admitting that everything happens within the conscious space of the self. It is within the self that the identity can exist and be observed, and it is the self that can get rid of it when it's limiting our potential and creating suffering.

As we get closer to merging with our self, the identity will try to steal our attention in any way it can. It will remind us of all the injustice and nastiness, which was done to us in childhood or with previous partners, only to bring us back into the trance of compulsive reactions. Once we observe that our identity loves to keep us trapped in past memories that are recycled again and again, blocking the natural evolution of the self, it becomes easy for us to regain our attention once more.

We are the self and we can easily, at any given moment, consciously win back the attention from the identity, instead of believing that the trance and illusion are real.

I want you to see that it is not as difficult as you might think to merge with your self, despite the mind's efforts to convince you of the contrary. Begin to question: *Who are you without your identity?* Ask yourself, "Who am I without my job, family, career, children, house, opinions, beliefs, body and mind?" It will likely be hard to see anything beyond these accumulated aspects of identity at first.

The identity, which manifests itself, and the self, which doesn't manifest itself, are in reality *one*. Better yet, they are two sides of the same coin.

The self is universal. It is naturally connected to all living creatures and it is our true nature, which includes everybody and everything. The identity, to the contrary, is exclusive. It wants to be different from everybody and everything, thus disconnecting us from existential life in favor of a psychological reality that pushes us more and more into loneliness.

In fact, the identity is in full opposition and resistance to its true nature, the all-inclusive self.

If we want to relate this to numbers, we can say that we are the zero from which all other numbers came to be, and that it becomes one within by transcending its illusory duality for the evolution of its own consciousness.

Oneness is the conscious realization of the divine and creative power within us, the unity between who we are, who we think and who we show ourselves to be.

It takes us a lifetime or longer to realize the unlimited possibilities of the entity we are, the self, from which and through which everything else manifests.

It is only our fear of standing there naked, without identity, that makes us blind to the truth.

The drop of water never asks itself who it is, it simply merges with the ocean. The same is true for us human beings.

The duality, separation and suffering we experience as the identity is only illusory; it comes from the mind's belief that it is a separate entity, disconnected from life itself.

We don't "do" or "have" life, *we are life*.

It's important to remember that the evolution of our

awareness is an endless journey. When we think we've got it, life will throw another challenging situation at us. The difference will be that with our enhanced awareness and perception, we will not suffer as much. It doesn't mean that we will not feel sadness or disappointment along the way—as long as we have a body and an identity, we will have emotions—but we will not end up as wounded anymore because by residing in our unshakable, peaceful and loving self, we will be stable enough to stand any situation without suffering unnecessarily.

Ninety percent of human suffering is caused by our identification with mind and identity; only a small percentage of life suffering comes from external situations, like tragedies or unavoidable natural catastrophes. This means that once we have broken the identification with our mind and identity, we are free from most suffering. Then we can face life without fear, exploring and expressing our endless potential.

May you spread your wings and become a creator with endless possibilities—the creator of the life you desire! May the story of my identity help you realize your authentic self!

AFTERWORD

THE SUBTLE PLAY OF LIFE AND DEATH

When I was in India, volunteering in the ashram school and learning yoga and meditation techniques, one day we were asked to consciously think about what we would do if this were our last day alive.

After this day, I began to live differently. For the first time, I became really conscious about the meaning of life and death. I came to understand that there is not something like life separated from death. Each time we breathe, we are living but at the same time we are also one moment nearer to death. We are living and dying every day. That's why it is essential to be aware of it and live fearlessly and with extreme gratitude each day of our life.

Living consciously means knowing that at some point in time we will have to give back our body to the earth and do it gracefully, because nothing belongs to us. This will be our last act of true awareness and acceptance of what is—awareness that the body will die while the self that we are will keep existing and evolving in the universe in different forms. I understood that we don't need to fear death, as it is the last natural step in a life lived in awareness. Life is death and death is life. There is life and life only!

Living with the fear of death or any other fear is non-living. It's a life that is not experiencing its full potential but just surviving within the limitations of its identity. It's a life that crawls instead of flying.

That's why I encourage you to go out and live fearlessly, with gratitude for the great gift that life is, the great gift that you are to the universe.

I kindly invite you to meditate in this direction and ask yourself:

If today were my last day on earth, what would I do? How would I love to be? What would I wish to leave behind?

You will be surprised by the insights this meditation can lead to.

After this meditation, we were asked to write a letter to the person we love most in life before leaving. I wrote the following letter to my daughter, which I would now like to extend to you with all my love.

Dear G.,

Before I go, I want to tell you that you are the most beautiful, unique piece of life I have ever seen on my earthly journey. You are my biggest love and the dearest person in my life. I wish that you will reside in the lap of grace every moment of your life and go through life in inner joy and happiness. Don't let yourself drag too much inside the meaningless and illusory thoughts self-created in your mind. Observe them, question them and drop them every time they don't serve you. Don't overestimate earthly bondages and material accumulations: boyfriends, money, jobs and family all are experiences that come and go; enjoy them without suffering.

Life comes with one certainty: Death. In the same way, all things are born to die and finish one day. This is the course of life. I know it sounds harsh, but I had to learn in life that the truth is not always nice. Know that only your body will perish; your self will keep living and being part of this universe. Live your life to the fullest and do what truly matters to you with full involvement and love.

I wish that you will find the right way to see life, and most of all, get to truly know and love yourself; touch the beauty of your true nature so you can stay away from suffering.

I bless you with the gift of awareness. May you learn to disengage from all the negative thoughts in your mind and see reality the way it is—from your heart, not from the distorted projections of mind.

One important thing: Don't take life and what you do too seriously. Bring humor and smile to every situation, because no matter what your mind makes you believe, earthly situations are not so important. Everything is happening in the right time at the right place. Know that.

Don't resist anything, whether it's bad or good. Accept all as life. The way you are while going through bad and good is what truly matters. Remember that life is generous and that everything is well in the here and now. Don't let your mind disturb this peace.

Every time you need help in life, look for help within your self; you have all the answers there. Sit in silence and look. Do yoga, meditate and your awareness will grow like a beautiful lotus flower from the mud of the mind and of all attachments.

I don't know if you can understand my words now; you will for sure say, "My 'spiritual' mama, once again." But one day you will, and I wish that for you as soon as possible.

In the meantime, if you should need me in your moments of deep despair, know that I will always be there, within and around you, loving you and supporting you in cooperation with the entire universe. Nothing and nobody will ever prevent me from loving you deeply. Not even you.

Live every moment of your life with full involvement but without entanglement. Get rid of all attachments—most of all, the attachment to your identity and thoughts, the false beliefs and concepts about yourself and others that don't serve your happiness.

Be joyful from within! Simply *be*!

You have the power to do it. You can create your happiness from within, no matter what troubles the situations outside may cause you. You can create the life you desire for yourself. Listen to your true essence and follow your pure intelligence within, which is free from tendencies, memories and thoughts.

Most of all, get rid of all fears by recognizing the loving, radiant, powerful and unshakable being you are. Love yourself and stay true to your authentic nature; this is the greatest secret, but not in an exclusive, egoistical way. Include everything and everybody within your love.

We have infinite love inside. Be one with everything and everyone and happiness will be what you will experience.

I love you a lot. Always love and protect your children and give them presence and love every day. Accept them as they are. Have no expectations of any kind. Never judge or reject them.

I hope that they will love you exactly the way you are. But even if they are confused, unaware and judging, keep loving them.

Be who you authentically want to be. Don't care about people's judgments and thoughts, as people will not die in your place, so they shall let you live the way you want. Do what you truly love and what matters to you. See that everything you do is connected to your wellbeing and the wellbeing of others and the planet.

Most importantly, express your limitless potential to the fullest. You can be and do what you want. There are no limits except for those you set yourself in your mind! Don't believe in the limits set by your mind. You are a free being, simply express your potential to the fullest. Stop crawling! Spread your wings!

Don't waste your time with anger, frustration, depression, judgments and criticism. Invest in joy, freedom, peace, love and compassion, as life is a very short journey.

Whenever you need a hand, I will be there to protect and guide you.

But always remember that the answers are within you, between the words written on a page, in the silence between a noise and the other, in the space between the walls of your room. Words, noise and walls are the limited perception of your mind. Go beyond them and you will find what truly matters: The joy and freedom of simply being the graceful and powerful piece of life that you are.

Love, light and laughter,

Your mum

Paola

ACKNOWLEDGEMENTS

Writing this book has been a little journey within the journey and I want to express my gratitude to everyone who was involved, directly or indirectly, in its manifestation.

To my daughter Giada, who is my best friend and most sincere mirror; she is the one who always gave me the strength to carry on and who loves me and accept me for who I am. She always supported me and my decisions and she encouraged me to write this book. I thank you for simply *being* the beautiful soul that you are!

I unconditionally love you and I always will.

To my mentor, Sadhguru Jaggi Vasudev, who I found at exactly the moment when I was seeking transformation. He is the founder of inner engineering and the most graceful being I had the honor to know in the course of my life. He is the one who helped me break the conditioning of my identity, my old thought patterns and inspired me to unfold my limitless possibilities, becoming the creator of the life I always desired, in awareness, with a vision, and in love and inclusiveness with all that is. Even when I was not in India, his presence was always with me, guiding me and helping me to get in touch and reside in the space of my true self. Thank you for making me understand whatever is and whatever is not.

Thank you for having included me and made me taste the beauty of living "in the lap of grace." I love you and hold you in deep esteem.

To R. – what can I say? You know me better than anybody and your straight spirit speaks directly to my self. The universe conspired to bring us together at the perfect time. I thank you for all the beautiful moments of pure, exuberant life we had together. But most of all I thank you for all the sad, "foggy" moments, as through them I got to understand so many things about myself and life. You were always a merciless mirror and an intrinsic part of my journey.

If you truly want to love somebody, love yourself first. Now I know. Thank you from the bottom of my heart for being always there for me.

To my best friend and sister Orietta, who was at my side at every phase of my life, including when I was a mess! A true, strong, friendship tightens me to her and I am grateful every day to have her as an integral part of my life. Thank you for our talks about the book, for the understanding I received so many times and for the useful advice you gave me. I feel blessed to have you as my best friend.

Thank you to my beloved Floriana. You are proof that there is no need to be blood sisters to always be there for each other. You are the water in the desert to me, and a safe port to which I can always return. Your capacity to love and include in your simple way is just beautiful. Your presence is a gift to me; our conversations an eye-opener and a good inspiration for parts of this book. I love you a lot.

To my editor, Chandika Devi, who perfectly grasped the essence of my manuscript and help me to convey it to its best.

Her loving and light-full self will transpire through this book, making it an even greater conductor for Oneness. Thank you from the bottom of my heart.

Thank you to Balboa Press and Hay House. It is an honor to be part of the Balboa Press/Hay House family. I am sure our cooperation will grow stronger and stronger.

A special thanks to Reid Tracy and his "author family", who gave me and many new authors like me useful and sincere tips about the world of writing & publishing during the Writer's Workshop. Most of all, thank you for strengthening us in our vision to be of service to the wellbeing of all human beings.

Last but not least, a loving tap on my shoulder and a special thank you to myself for the courage I have as I seek the truth, for the sincerity with which I look at myself and others, for the perseverance that helps me to not give up the search, even in the most confusing moments. I thank for every single person who will find shelter in the contents of my book and will be helped by it, and for everyone I could help thus far just by being who I am.

I thank each Mauritian sunset, the soft ocean breeze and the calmness of the ocean, which were my constant companions during my writing. Also, I lovingly remember Princess, the now-deceased dog who sat every day in the garden near the pool at the foot of my chair while I was writing what now has become this book. She accompanied me with her presence, reminding me constantly that we are all one!

ABOUT THE AUTHOR

Paola Corinaldesi was born in Rome, Italy and moved to Munich at the age of 23, where she lived for most of her life.

She got a bachelor in Arts at the University "La Sapienza" in Rome and due to her background, she is a multilingual talent, speaking Italian, English, German and Spanish fluently.

Paola worked in the corporate world for many years, mainly in the areas of Change Management / Training & Consulting, before deciding to take a break from her job and dedicate more time to herself and her true passion: Writing. She moved to Mauritius and spent almost three years there. It was during this time in Mauritius that this book came to be.

Triggered by some crucial experiences in her life, Paola underwent a total transformation from a person imprisoned in her psychological reality, with subconscious false beliefs and mental patterns governing her life, to a free and joyful being. She broke free from the conditioning of her mind and identity, from all attachments and unnecessary suffering, to transform herself into the creator of the life she desired.

Her transformation was slow and steady, culminating in a turning point at the ashram of the ISHA Foundation in

Coimbatore, India. Here, the author volunteered in a children's school as she was trained in a powerful yoga and meditation method for inner transformation.

Paola gives the wisdom of a lifetime and the results from her path of transformation with all her heart through this book, which is offered to everybody who is open and ready for it.

Reborn as the Self explains simple but powerful principles of spirituality in connection to true life experiences and situations, bringing them down to earth and offering practical means to manage a fulfilled and magical life.

The author is convinced that the biggest gift we can give ourselves and humanity is to make ourselves into joyful, free and peaceful beings who can manage our body, mind and energies into a stable, clean construct. Inner Management is a powerful way to reach the fulfillment of our unlimited possibilities as human beings in life, and a must in the evolution-path of all human beings.

In the author's opinion, no major changes can happen on the outside (world peace, religious conflicts, hunger) unless we first manage our inside. This book is her small contribution to that management.

Paola currently lives between Munich and Mauritius. When she is not travelling and busy with her second passion, pattern & fashion design, she teaches Inner Management in cooperation with many beautiful beings, who, like her, have a vision: Helping people to escape the prison of suffering and become the creator of the authentic life they long for.

Visit Paola on her Website: www.paolacorinaldesi.com

APPENDIX I: FINDING A YOGA CENTER

I am convinced that Yoga and meditation will be *the* technology of the future and I would like to explain why, through the beautiful and true words of Abdul Kalam, the eleventh president of the republic of India:

"Where there is righteousness in the heart, there is beauty in the character. When there is beauty in the character, there is harmony in the home. When there is harmony in the home, there is order in the nation. When there is order in the nation, there is peace in the world." - A. P. J. Abdul Kalam

Since it is both a technology and the science of the future, it is essential that yoga is properly transferred to students by the right teacher, in a conducive atmosphere.

I would like to underline that choosing the wrong teacher or center could produce counterproductive results, causing damage to your body and system. After all, yoga means union and alignment of body, mind and energy and every posture, breathing technique and meditation must be learned accurately.

Be aware that not every center in the West is equipped with the right knowledge to teach the science of yoga as transmitted by the ancient Vedic culture. Most of them have transformed the technology of yoga in a fashionable gym event.

On the other side, yoga is spreading off in all urban centers and luckily, more and more centers are connected with centers in the East, offering strong options for powerful teaching.

If you are not sure about your choice for a yoga center or you need any other information around yoga and meditation, I offer myself as a reliable source to support you finding the right Inner Management practices and tools.

You can either contact me via email at:
paolacorinaldesi@icloud.com
Or visit my website at:
paolacorinaldesi.com

Love, light & laughter,
Paola

Printed in the United States
By Bookmasters